RUSSELL TARG

NEW THINKING ALLOWED DIALOGUES

Russell Targ:
Ninety Years of Remote Viewing, ESP, and Timeless Awareness

JEFFREY MISHLOVE

www.whitecrowbooks.com

New Thinking Allowed Dialogues: Russell Targ.

A CIP catalogue record for this book is available from the British Library.
For information, contact White Crow Books by e-mail: info@whitecrowbooks.com.

Cover Design by Jana Rogge & Astrid@Astridpaints.com
Interior design by Velin@Perseus-Design.com

Paperback: ISBN: 978-1-78677-260-2
eBook: ISBN: 978-1-78677-261-9

Non Fiction / Body, Mind & Spirit / Parapsychology /
ESP, Clairvoyance, Precognition, Telepathy.

www.whitecrowbooks.com

Russell Targ, 2012.

Books Authored by Russell Targ:

Third Eye Spies: Learn Remote Viewing from the Masters
The Reality of ESP: A Physicist's Proof of Psychic Abilities
Do You See What I See: Memoirs of a Blind Biker
Limitless Mind: A Guide to Remote Viewing and Transformation of Consciousness
The End of Suffering: Fearless Living in Troubled Times, with J. J. Hurtak
The Heart of the Mind: How to Experience God Without Belief, with Jane Katra
Miracles of Mind: Exploring Nonlocal Consciousness and Spiritual Healing, with Jane Katra
The Mind Race: Understanding and Using Psychic Abilities, with Keith Harary
Mind at Large: Institute of Electrical and Electronics Engineers Symposium on the Nature of Extrasensory Perception with Charles Tart and Harold Puthoff
Mind Reach: Scientists Look at Psychic Ability with Harold Puthoff

Other books by Jeffrey Mishlove on the *New Thinking Allowed Dialogues* imprint:

Is There Life After Death?
UFOs and UAP: Are we Really Alone?

CONTENTS

A Note from Jeff

The first time I met Russell Targ was at the 1973 Convention of the Parapsychological Association in Charlottesville, Virginia. At the time, I was just starting my career as a graduate student at the University of California, Berkeley, with an independent doctoral major in Parapsychology. Russell had already achieved national media attention by then for his research with the controversial Israeli psychic, Uri Geller. I remember our first conversation vividly.

"How much did you pay Uri Geller for a day in your laboratory?" I naïvely asked. "That's none of your business," he replied. So, from the very beginning, Russell for me was a tall, intimidating, and almost unapproachable figure. A decade later, however, after Russell left SRI International, we became the best of friends—visiting each other on a regular, almost weekly, basis for a period of nearly twenty years (until I moved out of California in 2001).

After I established the *New Thinking Allowed* channel on YouTube, Russell came to visit me in Las Vegas, which is where we conducted the first seven of the fifteen interviews that have been transcribed, edited, and presented in this book.

To prepare the verbatim, spoken word transcripts for publication, it was necessary to edit them so that they would make sense on the written page. *The New Thinking Allowed* Foundation is very grateful for the work of our volunteer editors and designers (Greta Peavy, Elizabeth Lord, Jana Rogge, Laura Neubert, and Emmy Vadnais)—without whose generous help this book would not exist. Furthermore, as the interviews were spread out over a period of years, there were naturally instances when important episodes were told and retold. For the purposes of a book, that would not do.

My responsibility has been to remove repetitive material while, at the same time, making sure that each event discussed is presented as fully as possible. I hope that we accomplished this task smoothly. However, if the text appears either repetitive or disjointed in places, the fault is mine alone.

Throughout our conversations, Russell frequently references the work of other scholars and scientists. During the actual *New Thinking Allowed* videos, it has been our habit when guests make such identification to show a book cover written by or about the person under discussion. In this volume, however, we have presented neither book covers, nor bibliographical references. Curious readers, of course, can refer to the original videos that remain online in the *New Thinking Allowed* archives. Overall, what this book offers to readers is a window inside the mind of one of the most accomplished and successful parapsychological investigators of the twentieth century.

Foreword

Russell Targ and I met in 1977 through an introduction arranged by Ingo Swan whom I had also just met. That summer, when we were introduced, I was preparing to carry out a series of submarine experiments known as Project Deep Quest, thanks to the Institute of Marine and Coastal Studies at the University of Southern California and a Canadian submersible manufacturing company Hyco, Ltd, making a research submersible available to me. I had been planning this study for several years. But where does one get a submarine? Deep Quest sought to definitively establish using protocols I had been working with for almost a decade to determine whether or not nonlocal perception was electromagnetic in nature as had been posited by a number of researchers, particularly Michael Persinger at Laurentian University in Canada.

To answer this, I was using the consensus protocol I had designed to locate a previously unknown shipwreck on the ocean floor within the submersible's range limit off the coast of Santa Catalina Island where the submersible was doing its sea trials. That is, to penetrate the ocean beyond the depth where *em* radiation could obtain useful data, and then, using the Associated Remote Viewing (ARV) protocol that I had been working with, to put two remote viewers, one at a time, at a depth beyond *em* radiation and see if they could describe where target individuals were hiding hundreds of miles away.

At the last minute there was a crisis that threatened the entire project. The two viewers I was planning to work with, Alan Vaughan and George McMullen, notified me that they could not participate. Alan had come down with a very nasty flu, and George, who worked as the parts manager of a Chrysler dealership in Nanaimo, Canada, had a colleague whose pregnant wife made a premature delivery and took leave to take care of his wife; so George could not come down to Los Angeles.

Ingo had just introduced me to Russell, Ed May, Hal Puthoff, and Hella Hammid. The team of researchers and viewers that made up the SRI facility who were doing research similar to my own. At the last minute I asked Hella and Ingo whether they would substitute for Alan and George, and asked Russell and Hal whether they would be the outbound targets. When they said yes, I asked Ed whether he would be the monitor for the viewer interviews, since he was already familiar with working with them whereas I had just met them. As history knows, everything worked even better than any of us had hoped. And out of all that began a series of friendships, particularly with Hella and Ingo until they died, and with Russell.

Russell and I liked each other from the moment we met, and I quickly developed great respect for his intellect, his writing skills, and his understanding of nonlocal perception. For several years we taught a workshop together at the Omega Institute. Russell started what became a very important small invitational conference at the Esalen Institute, and, when he had to stop, he passed it on to me.

As I write this, we have been friends for almost half a century: 47 years. We visit each other, and talk and trade emails regularly. We test research ideas with each other and assess research by others. We have also helped each other through family tragedies and triumphs. Each of us has gone through the loss of a beloved wife, and Russell had also lost a daughter, Elizabeth, herself a significant researcher. We both love cats, and we share all sorts of little life patterns that make up enduring friendships.

If you look at the literature of parapsychology over the last century it immediately becomes clear that although it is not a large field, those who are the real thinkers and leaders in the discipline comprise an even smaller group, perhaps a dozen or so, who have made the really meaningful contributions to this science. Russell is one of them. His books, his papers and his lectures, stand out in a rare way. Before becoming involved in consciousness research he was a pioneer and leader in laser research. Through his connection with space pioneer Werner Von Braun he was able to get the initial funding that made the SRI project possible. He is a leader respected by everyone in the field, and I am grateful that he has been my friend and occasional colleague through the years. Anyone interested in getting real knowledge about remote viewing would be well advised to read his many books. He comes from a family background in publishing, and he also used those skills to locate long out of date works, sort out their copyrights, and republish, *Studies in Consciousness*, which I consider one of the most important series of books covering not just remote viewing, but the full range of really significant work carried out by researchers around the world.

In total, Russell is one of the most important figures in 20th and 21st century consciousness research.

Stephan A. Schwartz
Langley, Washington

PREFACE

The Birthday Party from Hell

I think that Aries people pay more attention to their Springtime birthdays than other people. But I could be wrong. On April 11, 2023, I arranged to have a small birthday party for my 89th birthday. This was the first meeting of any kind that I had attended in three years, because of Covid. I have congestive heart failure, so I can no longer run the Bay to Breakers foot race in under an hour. But I can walk around the neighborhood using walking sticks so that I don't fall on my ass on a pinecone. We had nine people at our dining room table for this celebration. There were my two sons, Alex a physician and Nicholas who is an attorney, and their wives, and my darling wife Patty, and Alex's daughter Sonia, who just graduated from medical school. Everyone at the table came down with very serious Covid. I wound up in the hospital for ten days with Bacterial Pneumonia, just as I feared.

But I soon came home and was back at my keyboard preparing for a Zoom interview to promote my new book, "Third Eye Spies", about my research as a physicist studying ESP for the CIA. Patty said that I reminded her of the famously resilient Energizer bunny who always pops up after he is knocked down. In our twenty years of married life, Patty has unfortunately seen me do this trick many times. Too many times. She reminded me that I had a lifetime of legal blindness, cancer, breathing problems and all kinds of crazy mishegoss. Since I had already published ten books, she thought it might be interesting to write a book about my life as the resilient Blind biker, whom you will meet shortly.

"Many Lives of the Blind Biker"
by Russell Targ

1. Bloody Chicago

I am an American physicist born in Chicago in 1934 at Woodlawn Hospital on April 11th during a rare spring blizzard. And I was almost killed that same day in a botched bris carried out by a shaky Moyle who had no way of knowing that his patient had a rare bleeding disorder that immediately filled the room with blood and confusion. The Moyle left the premises, and my parents shortly found an intern who had no problem stitching up the squalling baby.

2. What else could go wrong?

My vision went wrong. It turned out that this large healthy baby boy had a congenital disorder known as Hermansky-Pudlak Syndrome which provides almost no pigmentation to the macular region of the retina, which is normally the center of most acute vision. Also unfortunately, in Hermansky-Pudlak the platelets don't coagulate making hemorrhaging a constant threat. So that's the origin story of The Blind Biker and the dreadful badge of "legally blind." But somehow that Blind Biker was able to ride his Honda Nighthawk 35,000 miles through the Foothills of Silicon Valley.

3. What's to become of him?

I was an only child, and my parents were very concerned about my future. A variety of well-wishing prognostications from relatives and guidance counselors ran the gamut from institutionalization to farmer!

4. What to do?

My mother, Anne Targ, was a newspaper columnist, and she provided her eager three-year-old with giant hand-made flash cards made from shirt cardboards. This intervention, together with a steady diet of readings from "The Little Engine That Could," had me reading big print by the time I entered kindergarten. We also had frequent swimming outings to beautiful Oak Street Beach on Lake Michigan near our home.

Russell Targ at his best, Oak Street Beach, Chicago, 1937.

Things were going well in the first grade of the Kozminski Elementary School. In the second grade your author met a calamity. All of the in-class exams were prepared by the teacher on the blackboard. Though I was always sitting in the first row of our 5 x 7 row classroom, I could not come close to reading anything on the blackboard from my desk. The teacher accommodated her "near-sighted" problem-child by allowing me to parade back and forth in front of the classroom and copy the questions into my notebook, and then return to my desk to write the essay or solve the problem. This eight-year-old public humiliation was so traumatic that it was part of my dream life for decades after. Later, I learned about lucid dreams, and the traumatic dreams went away.

5. More blood spilled.

This is 1940 and there is still no good cure for tonsillitis. After several infections, I was scheduled to have my tonsils removed. What could go wrong? After many minutes of ether anesthesia, I found myself floating near the ceiling of the operating room, looking down on the top of filthy lamps, a tray full of blood and shiny steel instruments. I have since learned that this kind of out-of-body experience is not even unusual during ether anesthesia.

I remember being returned to my room and my waiting mother, and hearing the doctor tell her that he can't sew me up. He said, "It's like trying to sew up scrambled eggs." And with that he left the hospital, to leisurely spit into the Chicago wind, and mess his tie, according to my mother's report. Once again, we were able to find a hospital resident who successfully sewed me up. Hermansky-Pudlak syndrome would not be discovered until 1959, late, but not too late for me, as it turned out.

6. Pearl Harbor.

Good news for the Jews. On Sunday, December 7th, 1941, the little Targ family was having lunch in a favorite, basement Chinese restaurant on the North Side of Chicago. It's a memorable occasion for me because it was the day I was introduced to delicious lychee nuts, and also learned to eat with chopsticks. Not an easy task for a south paw, because your teacher is right-handed.

As we left the restaurant in my father's Chevy coup, we heard on the radio that the Japanese had attacked Pearl Harbor. My father's response was to call out, "Thank God. Finally, Roosevelt will declare war on the Nazis." Roosevelt had recently turned back the ship, St. Louis, full of Jewish refugees, because the Republicans felt that "America already had enough Jews." This was the ship that carried my father's parents to America in 1906, escaping the pogroms in Krakow, Poland. My father's feelings were strongly echoed at a Sunday chicken dinner with his extended family and his mother, whom I recognized as Grandma Bubby. My mother was present, but not especially welcomed because of her mother's Christmas tree. Her mother was known to me as Grandma Tilly, an enthusiastic Christian Scientist.

7. Targ's Book Shop.

My father was an indefatigable reader with a prodigious intellect. In spite of this, he failed to graduate from his high school in the far corner of the Jewish West Side of Chicago. He won an essay contest which led him to his first job selling books from city to city for McMillan Book Company, who encouraged him to change his name from Torgownik to something more pronounceable, like Targ. He soon became an editor, and the following year he bought his first book shop on the West Side. That did very well, and he moved to downtown Chicago in the Loop.

William and Anne Targ, at Targ's Chicago Book Shop.

This shop became a favorite meeting spot, a salon for many of Chicago's most famous writers, who stayed with him, as he became Editor-in-Chief for G. P. Putnam's in New York. These included Mario Puzo, who wrote the *Godfather*, McKinley Cantor, who won a Pulitzer Prize for "Andersonville", Richard Wright, and James T. Farrell. I was very fortunate to have friendly contact with many of these great writers, when we moved to New York.

Next door to the Chicago bookstore was a small shop selling "tricks and jokes," and simple books on magic; just the thing for an eight year old. My father also had magic books on his shelves, and he encouraged me with a large magic set featuring tough sleight-of-hand tricks, like "Cups and Balls" and Chinese linking rings. Eventually, I moved on to "card magic" at which I became very proficient. These experiences led to my life-long interest in magic. Every experienced magician knows that there is always a little room for ESP to slip into even the cheesiest card trick.

8. Moving on.

In 1942 my father was offered an editorial job with The World Publishing Company in Cleveland. His work there was so successful that he was invited to become a senior Editor and open a New York Office in The Time Life building in Rockefeller Center.

9. *Passing through Cleveland.*

Our family took the Pacemaker New York Central from Chicago to Cleveland, the beginning of my love affair with trains. We rented a large three-story wooden farmhouse on Euclid Heights Boulevard. This was a big change from our small Chicago flat across from an orphanage off busy 63rd Street. My Father spread out his large library on the first floor and I gradually assembled an electric train layout that ran from room to room on the otherwise empty third floor. This was very valuable hands-on training for an aspiring physicist with not very good vision.

10. *Sight-saving classes.*

The Cleveland school system put me in a class for the visually handicapped. The teacher typed up our books into 16-point Bulletin size print. My father brought home a similar machine for me, so that I could easily read what I typed for class. In this one-room school for all grades, the teacher, Ada Baker, read the material to all classes, and everyone was welcome to sit in on all classes. For an auditory learner like me this was a Godsend. I entered fourth grade, skipped the fifth, and left the school having completed three grades in two years. I was able to do the same trick again, when I entered sight-saving class in New York the following year. This allowed me to enter high school at twelve and college at sixteen. But I still didn't have glasses that would allow me to read normal print. That would not come until bifocals in college.

World Publishing was owned by Ben Zevin, who inherited this large bible and dictionary company from his wife's family. Zevin hired my father as an editor to expand the company into the fiction and non-fiction trade market in which my father was a renowned expert. My ten-year-old understanding of the situation was that Zevin was jealous of my father's prowess and reputation and retaliated by paying him a sub-minimum wage. For some reason, my mother had to do the family shopping on a budget of $2.00 per day, which took an enduring terrible toll on her mental and physical health. The main thing I learned in Cleveland was that I didn't ever want to be poor.

11. 1945.

In 1945, my father was offered the editor-in-chief job, and we moved to a spacious second floor walk-up, apartment on 8th street in thriving and exciting Greenwich Village, across from the Whitney Museum of American Art. I was able to go swimming in the beautiful fountain in Washington Square Park.

12. Rolling down Christopher Street.

P.S. 3 (Public School 3) was not the closest school to our apartment, just off Fifth Avenue, but it had a Sight-Saving class, similar to what I found so helpful in Cleveland. It was an enormous five-story brick building with all nine grades under one roof. It was about a mile from my home, at the far end of Christopher Street, near the Hudson River. I was eleven and entered P.S.3 in the seventh grade and skipped the eighth grade the following year to set me up to enter high school. But I was still a long way from owning a bicycle. My parents didn't want me to be pedaling a bike in New York City traffic. Eight years later I would be riding my English three-speed from the Village to Columbia University at 120th street and Broadway. But in 1945, it was roller skating or take the bus.

I would roller skate most days with good old-fashioned steel-wheeled skates. Christopher Street was the heart of Greenwich Village. On the corner of Sixth Avenue was the 10th Street coffee emporium, with fresh ground coffee from all over the world. All this was of great interest to my coffee-loving parents. One block down was Bleaker Street, with a huge, arching cheese store that would fill the whole neighborhood with its aroma. On the corner of Seventh Avenue was the Village Vanguard where Odetta, the great (six feet tall) folk singer might be practicing for her evening show. Across from my school was the refurbished Theatre de Lys, which had brought Bertolt Brecht's "The Three Penny Opera" to New York with Lotte Lenya returning as the star. I saw this adaption of "The Beggar's Opera" many times during its long run.

In my new sight-saving class, we still had all grades together and everyone had his or her own typewriter. We were expected to learn to touch-type. Our very friendly teacher again typed up all our materials and we were expected to march through the halls and matriculate with our regular grades, making sure that we grabbed a front row seat, though I could never see the blackboard in any classroom situation. This did me in at Columbia, where the distinguished Prof. T. D. Lee had no textbook and no notes except the blackboard notes which he made up as he went along.

13. *School On Ice.*

During our lunch break, many of us would walk down to the river for fresh air and to enjoy the view. Some of us would buy a hotdog with mustard and sauerkraut and a chocolate egg-cream (soda) from a pushcart vender. We could then take the Hoboken Ferry across the river, round-trip for just a nickel. In the winter, the river would sometimes be choked with ice, stopping the ferry in its tracks, until the harbor police would shake it loose. Of course, we could hardly be blamed for missing our first afternoon class. It was sort of an act of God.

14. *Youth Builders.*

Our dinner table conversation was always stimulated by stories from my father about the geo-politics of running a publishing company in the Post War era. Communists, homosexuals, anti-Semites, and racism were always on deck, stimulated by my father's friendship with the famous black writer Richard Wright, and his good Chicago pal, the red-tinted writer James T. Ferrell. So, when my history teacher mentioned that the school was going to propose some students to take part in a "Youth Builder" current events program, supported by NBC and its well known commentator Bill Slater, I was ready to go. In fact I got along so very well with Bill Slater, as a twelve year old rabble rouser, that the show kept me for a full semester, to talk about the cases of juvenile delinquency, which was a big problem on the streets of New York at that time, just before "West Side Story." None of this made me very popular with the Italian gangs in my school, who were never very sympathetic toward a tall, near-sighted Jew on roller-skates.

15. *Museum of Natural History.*

Somehow it was arranged that all the students who were going to skip eighth grade, would do their last semester entirely at the New York Museum of Natural History. We learned to make things out of clay and fire them in a large kiln. We visited all the large dioramas with guides and spent several days looking at stars at the Hayden Planetarium. We toured their extensive collection of amazing jewels, and a full museum wing of ancient Egyptian reconstructions. I was especially fascinated by several displays showing the day-by-day embryonic development of birds and chicks starting with a tiny, fertilized embryo and ending with the full-sized animal. So orderly. Where could that order come from?

The Hall of Who We Are.

16. Leaving P.S. 3.

P.S. 3 treated me very well as a handicapped student from another city. They arranged for me to skip a grade, gave me an opportunity to be a child broadcaster, and sent me to a world-class museum for a semester. But they fell down in the department of guidance. The problem was what to do about my vision without any sight-saving class. We consulted with a noted New York ophthalmologist, who suggested we look into New York's schools for the blind. He wasn't stupid. He just didn't understand the unnamed cause of my poor vision. Things are not out of focus for me. All I need is a ton of magnification, and I can then read whatever is in front of my nose. Nothing is going to let me read the blackboard, short of powerful binoculars. I used these in graduate school.

The conclusion with all the counselors was that I should go to an agricultural high school and train to be a farmer! This neglects the fact that I have serious albinism, which greatly reduces my vision in bright sunlight. But the decision was made, much to my father's disappointment, that I should go to Newton agricultural High School in the Borough of Queens. But, like so many crazy decisions in my life script, this also had a surprisingly good outcome. We gave up our Greenwich Village apartment and moved to Queens, much to my father's discomfort, since he now had to take the elevated train daily to reach his office in the City. We returned to Fifth Avenue eight years later.

17. Why are there chickens flying round in the basement? You guessed it, Targ did it.

Newtown had substantial Biology, Chemistry, and Physics labs that were used to prepare the various experiments, which students would set up and carry out during the New York State Regents curriculum. This curriculum prescribed three one year courses, each ending with a comprehensive three-hour exam that must be passed by any New York State student who hopes to go to college with science credits. Newtown also had large operating farms in Flushing. Years later I rode by it on my bicycle, on my way to Brookhaven National Labs miles away.

Shortly after starting Newton, I was assigned to the required first year biology class. I took that opportunity to offer my services to help in the biology prep lab. The cheery short woman who ran the lab was happy to have a freshman volunteer who could reach all the top shelves. After a couple of weeks in the lab, I proposed to the manager, Mrs. Marinoff, that I would like to create a full set of chick embryo whole mounts as they have at the Natural History Museum. She said yes that she could get me two-dozen freshly fertilized eggs from the farm in Flushing. I think she admired the thirteen-year-old punk in front of her. But she suggested that I should have an upperclassman, who could better see what she was doing, to work with me. My new partner was Cynthia Goldwasser, a junior level biology student. We were given a spot to work in a corner of the school's basement. We then carefully placed our eggs, one-by-one, onto the large incubator that we were given from the farm. Everybody wanted this project to work. Day by day we would carefully crack open an egg and look for activity. At the end of two weeks, we were developing a nice display of chick-embryo development whole mounts. Each was carefully dipped into its own small container of formaldehyde. At the end of a little less than two weeks we heard some cracking when we opened the incubator door.

We took out the eggs and watched them hatch. We kept the two fledglings in a box and fed them grain. At the end of three days, they were beginning to wiggle their wings and, on day four, they took off out of their box. We named them Goldy and Max, and we had lots of visitors to help us chase the baby flyers. By the end of the week, they were sent back to the farm, presumably for a long and happy life. The set of whole mounts had a proud position in the biology lab at least for my three years at Newton. But that was not the high point of my first year of High School Biology.

18. My first contact with Parapsychology.

In my first week of high-school biology, we were learning to look through microscopes at tiny creatures like Paramecia, Spyro Gyra, and Ameba. It turns out that I have no trouble at all seeing things with a microscope (or a telescope for that matter.) On Friday afternoon, as we were putting our equipment away, our teacher, Mrs. Wells, introduced a tall very well-dressed upper class man to our assembled class.

He was Robert Rosenthal who had just come back from a meeting of the Parapsychology Association at the Rhine Research center at Duke University. Rhine was interested in studying how some people can see into the distance or into the future. This sounded to me like real magic, unlike the fake magic I had been using for several years to entertain people. What could be of greater interest to a visually handicapped Seventh grader?

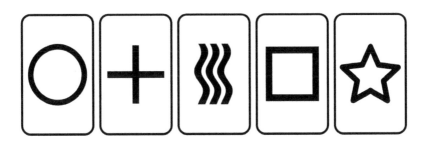

These cards were used for years in Rhine's lab
for statistical testing ESP.

These are the famous Zener cards that J. B. Rhine used for decades to investigate psychic abilities at Duke University. Rosenthal passed around several decks of the magical cards allowing groups of students to test their ESP. I immediately got the picture. Where could I buy the cards? Nothing could be simpler. I could just take the subway to the American Society for Psychical Research on 73rd Street and Central Park West. By Saturday afternoon, I had the cards in my hand, and made friends with the women who ran the American Society for Psychical Research, ASPR in New York. They were very generous to the skinny kid with glasses in front of them. They gave me several past volumes of their journal, and a copy of J.B. Rhine's recent book, "The Reach of the Mind." In my own ESP research, years later, I never used these cards. I much preferred pictures or objects which are less likely to encourage guessing. I used pictures and geographic targets successfully to teach remote viewing for the next sixty years.

Robert Rosenthal went on to become a distinguished Harvard Psychology professor. He famously demonstrated that even the most careful experimental psychologists could accidentally distort the outcomes of their experiments to obtain a desired result. For example, he showed that randomly selected "late bloomers" for IQ, were found to have greatly increased IQ at the end of the semester.

At the end of the flying chickens caper, I realized that I wasn't that interested in getting acquainted with small animals, and I was quite unsuited to research that involved looking at tiny embryos or anything else through a microscope.

With the urging of a physics student friend in my biology class, I found my way to the physics preparation laboratory on the second floor, where all the demonstration experiments were conceived and assembled by a brilliant teacher, Abraham Marcus, who wrote the "Basic Electricity" book for the U.S. Army signal Corps during WWII. He was not allowed to teach in the high school because he had a "Yiddish" accent. That is, he was born on the Lower East Side of New York. We were fighting the Nazis, but there was still plenty of antisemitism to go around. It was Abe Marcus, more than any other teacher, who set my sails in the direction of a life of hands-on experimental physics, and it was in the optics preparation part of my second semester that I realized that I could add a separate 9 diopter lens to my 7 diopter spectacles, and thereby create a 4-power magnifier, with which I could read ordinary text! I am not claiming to have invented the bifocal. Benjamin Franklin did that. But I now had the tools to convince a skillful Park Avenue optometrist that he should try to make me bifocals with a 9 diopter "add", which was new territory in 1950.

This was a good year for me. I turned sixteen, I could read my textbooks, I graduated from high school, and was accepted to Queens College, an easy bike ride from my home in Jackson Heights.

Four short years later, in 1954, I was graduated from Queens College with a degree in physics, and I was accepted to Columbia University Graduate physics department, with a full tuition assistantship. But, alas, my happy breeze though Queens College did not prepare me for all the Nobel Prize winners at Columbia.

I left Columbia in 1956 to join the Sperry Gyroscope Company, on Long Island. I worked there for two years under the direction of Dr. Morris Edinburgh who was the kind and brilliant director of their R&D Laboratory and also a Midrash teacher at the New York Hebrew Theological seminary. I often thought that he hired me to chat with him on his one-hour drive back and forth to Sperry. I was working on the design of high-power microwave tubes and electron discharge in gases for which I had no training, but I had read lots of philosophy.

In 1958, my good friend, Gordon Gould, from Columbia invited me to join his new company, Technical Research Group TRG Inc. which was going to pursue Gould's new idea of the LASER, for which he received a patent in 1977, after a long battle with Bell Labs. Gordon plucked me from obscurity to work on his brilliant invention because of our friendship and my experience with electron discharges in gases, which was crucial to early lasers. We did not build the first laser. This was accomplished by Ted Maiman, at Hughes Laboratory in California in May of 1960. I published my first laser paper with Gould in 1962. I published my last laser paper, describing my development of a 1000-watt CO_2 laser in 1969.

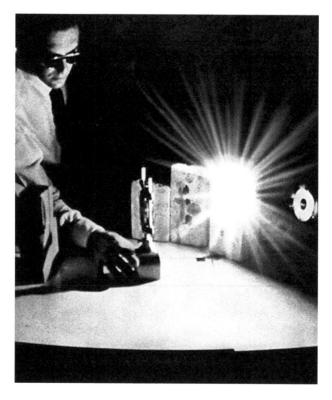

Russell Targ with his 1000 Watt laser.

1

Getting Started in Parapsychology

Recorded on March 2, 2017

Jeffrey Mishlove: Our topic today is getting started in parapsychology. I'm very honored to be with one of the world's premier parapsychologists, Russell Targ, who is the co-founder of the remote viewing program at SRI International. Russell is also a laser scientist and is the author of many books, including *The Reality of ESP, Do You See What I See?*—his autobiography—*Mind-Reach, The Mind Race, Mind at Large, Limitless Mind,* and *The Heart of the Mind.* Welcome, Russell.

Russell Targ: I'm happy to be here. It takes a physicist to write all these books about the mind.

Mishlove: It's a very interesting topic, and you've lived a fascinating life. I know that there will be young people reading this thinking maybe they'd like to have a career in parapsychology. I think it'll be very instructive to talk about how you began. In your case, it really goes back, in some ways, to your earliest childhood.

Targ: I grew up in Chicago and was interested in magic and tricks like every kid. My father was a bookseller in downtown Chicago, and next to his store was a tricks and jokes shop. My father would bring home little magic tricks such as how to make the penny disappear, or turn nickels into dimes, the sort of thing an eight-year-old can do. After I learned the trick, I would hand the apparatus back to my customer to fool them. Every kid likes to fool adults. From my earliest years, I was very interested in that kind of close-up table magic tailored for children.

At the age of about eight, we moved to Cleveland where I got a little more serious about learning magic. My father was publishing books by Thurston, who was an Ohio-based magician of some note, and I got to see the great Blackstone on the stage. My father and I got to talking about how he made a woman disappear. We didn't really know, but what must have happened? She didn't vaporize. Where could she have gone? I got the idea that you can use your analytical skill to decompose some of the things that seem magical. About that time, my father brought me a Blackstone magic kit with linking rings, cups, and balls; that kind of thing. I became a serious child magician, which I pursued for some time.

It was self-evident to me that we have psychic abilities. I remember, as an eight-year-old, I would play cards with my mother. I often knew what card was coming up next. I just took that ability for granted. I was a very successful card player. I didn't have a name for the skill. I sure didn't think I was psychic; I was just aware that I was a very fortunate card player. As a college student, I was playing duplicate bridge, where you and your partner will play against another couple. You must play according to specific rules. From time to time, the opponents would call the tournament director wanting to know if we had a secret code, because we were too successful in doing things that should be only 50-50. In bridge, they call it playing a 'finesse:' using a lower card to capture a higher value card. I was very successful in making the right choice with cards.

In the mid-1940s, we moved to New York, I was twelve years old then. I could go to 42nd Street and haunt the magic shops where professional magicians would buy their tricks. Down in the basement was Hubert's Museum and Flea Circus, and I could stand right in front of a magician doing tricks on a little table. All my life I've had very poor vision. So, it helped to stand right in front of a magician for as long as I wanted, paying a quarter to stay in this place all day if I wanted to. I could watch magic in the basement and then go up to the magic store to hobnob with the magician.

For several years, I performed magic on the stage in New York for birthdays or art openings and that sort of thing until I was fourteen years old.

My father had an interest in magic of the real kind, so his shop was full of magic books and books on Theosophy and other things like that, and rare books. He eventually moved our family to New York City, where he became vice president of G.P. Putnam's and published *The Godfather*. So, he was on a very good trajectory from his little bookshop in Chicago, and that moved us all to New York.

In New York, he was publishing books. I had a free run of the city. I could run off to Hubert's Flea Circus, which is an amusement building on 42nd Street. For a fourteen-year-old, I could go to Hubert's and see people doing sleight-of-hand magic right in front of me. My vision's not very good, as you recall. So, if I could stand in front of a guy at a card table all day long doing magic, I would get a very firsthand experience. I could then go upstairs in the building and talk to professional magicians and buy tricks across the counter.

By that time, I was fourteen, I was becoming an experienced, let's say, amateur magician doing stuff on the stage. Pretty good quality, too: linking rings; traditional magic tricks. I was doing this on stage.

In the same year, 1948, that Rosenthal introduced me to ESP cards was my last time on stage doing magic. I was fourteen years old, doing what became my regular shtick, which was a half a dozen, high quality, semi-sleight-of-hand magic tricks. People were very mystified because these are sort of tried-and-true big effects. I did this for a couple of hundred people at an art opening on Madison Avenue, where John Groth had just come back from the war, working with Ernie Pyle as war correspondents. Groth was a painter, and he was a friend of my father's. My father had published the collected paintings of John Groth.

At this art opening, I was the entertainment. After I had done my magic tricks, the author's wife, Ann, said, "We put all the entry tickets into a jar, here, and I'd like you to stir them up. We will give this beautiful painting of a soldier and a Dutch girl in the field to whoever's ticket you pull out," from a couple of hundred movie theater coupons or tickets. I reached in, I stirred them up and stirred them up. I can't read very well, so I gave the ticket to Ann. She said, "Here's a ticket, number 528761. Does anybody have that?" Everything got quiet, nobody had that. It occurred to me, well, I had one in my pocket. I pulled out mine and handed it to Ann, and she said, "By God, the young magician had the winning ticket." So, I had stirred up this pot of a hundred tickets and pulled out mine. They agreed that the magician could have this painting, which I have on my wall now.

But Ann said, "That's not fair. Somebody should be able to win this other than the magician. So, stir them up again, Russ, and pull out another ticket." I stirred them up again and gave Ann another ticket.

She read out a new number. Silence in the room. Finally, my father stood up from the back of the room and said, "Well, by golly, Russ did it again. He pulled out my ticket." So, the second picture, which is a beautiful color painting of a bullfight, I also have on my wall. I managed to pull out from a group of 200, I pulled out my ticket, my father's ticket, at odds of like one in 40,000. A very unlikely event.

Now, we like to believe we live in a causal world. I not only couldn't arrange the tickets, but I also couldn't even read the tickets. So, I'm totally innocent of any sleight of hand, but somehow, I was able to facilitate the outcome. I played a part, no doubt. I reached into the jar two times and pulled out our family's tickets two times with odds of one in 40,000. That was my last time on stage. I figured that was a magical occurrence. I was already now reading the *Journal of the Society for Psychical Research*, and I was moving out of stage magic.

That was a transformative experience for me because I realized that all my years of fake magic were in the background compared to people at Duke University doing the real magic. I threw away my childish stage magic materials and took the subway to the American Society for Psychical Research, located in Central Park South. They gave me a deck of ESP cards, and I subscribed to the society's quarterly journal, *American Society for Psychical Research*. As a fourteen-year-old high school junior, I was beginning to study what the real magicians were doing.

Mishlove: I understand, for the benefit of our readers, I don't think that journal is being published any longer.

Targ: No, they fell on hard times. They published for probably 75 years, and now the whole ASPR is probably out of business.

Mishlove: It's a shame. It had a wonderful history, if I recall correctly, William James, the great American psychologist, was one of the founders. In any case, you made the leap from fake magic to what we might call real magic.

Targ: I began to do experiments and to read about these kinds of things. As one of the advanced girls was giving a talk on the stage during physics club, I had a vision that someday I would be on that stage telling these people about psychic abilities. I recalled the vision years later when I was the one on stage.

Mishlove: A premonition.

Targ: It was a preview of what was going to happen later.

Mishlove: You were fortunate to live in New York City, where, in addition to the American Society for Psychical Research, there was also the Parapsychology Foundation.

Targ: And the Theosophical Society that we'll talk about later. In college, I was mainly concerned with playing bridge and studying physics, which were my two favorite things. I was always a very enthusiastic card player, and a tournament bridge player. I would often make bids just based on my impression of how things were going to turn out. I recall a tournament director wanting to know if we had a special, unannounced convention. My partner said, "I don't know what that guy is doing; he just does whatever he feels like, but we have no convention."

Mishlove: What is a convention?

Targ: A convention is a code between players like when I nod my head, it means spades. Or when I refold my hand, it means I've got hearts, even though I'm bidding diamonds. It's a secret trick, indicating other cards than the cards that you're allowed to say you have.

Mishlove: I see. So, bridge partners use these.

Targ: Secret conventions to communicate more data than they're allowed to.

Mishlove: I see. In other words, you were using your own intuition or ESP at that time.

Targ: That's right.

Mishlove: You're mostly known as a researcher, but you've had your share of psychic experiences and a certain level of ability as well.

Targ: I have memories of playing cards and just knowing which one was going to turn up next. You can use that in Las Vegas. For instance, if you're playing blackjack, you can bet more on the hands where you think you're going to win. Even if you have no ESP and you're betting more at random, it won't cost you anything. But, if you've got a small amount of ESP and you bet $20 on the hands you think you're going to win and $2 on the other hands, you wind up making a lot of money. You will also draw a crowd because people quickly attune to what's going on. It's a surprisingly effective strategy.

Mishlove: When J.B. Rhine, back in the 1930s, began doing ESP experiments at Duke University using a deck of Zener cards, he was, in effect, modeling a kind of experience that many people have playing bridge or poker or other games of that sort where they can profit from their ESP.

Targ: We now know that card guessing is a singularly difficult kind of ESP task to do rather than so-called free response tasks. If I was to ask you the number I'm thinking of from 1 to 10, you'd say, "Well, it's probably not a 1 or a 10 because he just said those and he probably wouldn't pick a 7 because it's everybody's lucky number." That's not psychic functioning, that's analysis. Whereas if I told you I'm visualizing some place on the planet that I know well but you've never seen, and then ask you about the place I'm visualizing. That's a very easy task. Even though I'm choosing my place from an infinite number of places, it's an easier task than guessing a number from 1 to 10. That was the work that we did at Stanford Research Institute for twenty years.

Mishlove: On the other hand, when you're playing bridge, you're not thinking about a forced-choice ESP test. It's a game. You're engaged in it.

Targ: What's going to show up in front of you?

Mishlove: It's a real-life situation. ESP experiments are contrived.

Targ: That's right. When I went to graduate school at Columbia to study physics, I was taken to a lecture at the Theosophical Society by one of my co-students. We heard about Bridey Murphy, who was a supposed reincarnated Irish woman who remembered a previous life. I met several of the Theosophical bigwigs at the time, including the psychic healer Dora Kunz, who ran the Theosophical Society. I became friends with her. If I hid a magnet in her office, she could find it because she had that psychic ability.

Mishlove: In other words, she was able to visualize the magnetic field.

Targ: Yes. I became very interested in the Theosophical Society. They owned an early copy of the Theosophical magazine with an article written by Annie Besant called "Occult Chemistry." When I was first a graduate student at Columbia, I got involved with the Theosophical Society in New York. I was twenty years old. I learned about this organization interested in psychic stuff. They had a beautiful home in midtown Manhattan. They frequently had lectures on fairies, psychic abilities, and the ancient wisdoms. You were encouraged to separate the good from the bad, the useful from the non-useful. Helena Blavatsky had a new spin on the Vedic tradition.

Mishlove: That's fascinating. Of course, the Theosophical Society is a very important organization in terms of the evolution of the whole consciousness movement and what has come to be known as New Age culture. It strikes me that the fundamental message of your documentary is that remote viewing is an ability available to virtually everybody.

I had been involved with the Theosophical Society for many years. Before that, I had been a kundalini meditator, reading Arthur Avalon's book, *The Serpent Power,* and trying to clear my mind, to live in loving-kindness, compassion, empathetic joy and equanimity to the four immeasurables that the Buddhists believe in, but also that was part of the kundalini. You want to learn to be a compassionate person and the dividend: you awaken your crown chakra to experience the cosmos. In kundalini you release the energy in your spine, supposedly. It goes up your spine and reaches your brain and awakens you to be able to see the universe. I was familiar with that. I did this for some years until, I discovered, they were right. You can really get into serious trouble if you meditate on these powerful forces without a teacher.

Mishlove: Annie Besant was one of the founders, along with Madame Blavatsky, of the Theosophical Society.

Targ: In theosophy, they believe you can experience the universe using direct perception, as a pantheistic view. In 1895, Madame Blavatsky had the idea that her two prodigious psychics, Charles Leadbeater and Annie Besant, could sit in front of a block of paraffin at the laboratory in Adyar, India, and describe the atoms. They started with hydrogen because that's the lightest one and were able to describe it using a peculiar ideographic form. There are two other kinds of hydrogen: one which they called "occultium," with one extra atomic unit in it, and "adyarium," named after the city that they were in. They had discovered two isotopes of hydrogen in the late eighteen hundreds, before the idea of isotopes even existed.

Mishlove: As a graduate student in physics at the time, you were able to recognize the significance.

Targ: I found that very exciting. I didn't understand all of Theosophy and their secret doctrine, but I understood that these people are on to something: that psychic abilities can go way beyond playing cards.

Mishlove: Although the Theosophical Society is a rather small and obscure movement today, historically speaking, they've had an enormous impact.

Targ: They still have a sizable following in England.

Mishlove: I think there are maybe 5,000 members in the United States today.

Targ: They published my last book, for example, *The Reality of ESP.*

Mishlove: Quest Books, their publishing arm.

Targ: Yes, and I thought that was nice. After graduating I left Columbia, and I had ideas for experiments. In general, I'm not the smartest guy around, but I often have good ideas for what to do.

Mishlove: You got involved in pioneering work in the field of lasers, at the very early stages when lasers were just being discovered.

Targ: Early in my laser career, I would drive back and forth to work with my boss, the head of the research laboratory at Sperry Gyroscope in Great Neck, Long Island. He was a very thoughtful man. He was a musician and he taught midrash, which is Talmud, at a theological seminary. He was not interested in the psychic stuff, but he was a man who held broad interests. As we were driving home once, I said, "Morris, I have this strange image that doesn't look like it's mine. I see an oval table with candlesticks. There's a book and it looks like black pages with white letters. Somebody has drawn green circles and red checks. It doesn't look like anything I've ever seen." I was not completely naïve. I'm aware of what psychic images look like and I've got a lot of experience. The key to recognizing a psychic image is to have it clear and bizarre and outside your normal experience. That is, if we're passing Flushing Meadows and I visualized a baseball diamond, that would not be very significant. Here I had a collection of images, which truly made no sense. They were outside of my experience, and I saw they were in Hebrew letters. I don't read Hebrew. He said, "My old friend Schreiber is often looking at manuscripts. He's a rabbi, and he's got a table like that." The next day I went to Morris' house, and he unrolled this manuscript. In fact, a photostat—which doesn't exist anymore—of a Hebrew document that Schreiber was annotating. It had the white Hebrew letters. If he liked the thing, and the way it was written, he would give it a green circle. If he thought it was wrong, he'd give it a red X. Basically,

I completely described this bizarre thing outside of my [experience]. In my life, from time to time, these unasked for, surprising images, are a key for me. They come to me by ESP. The problem with doing ESP experiments is, the thing the person imagines does not have a little tag on it saying, "This image is brought to you by ESP." That would be very nice, but we don't have that.

The question is, where did that come from? Morris immediately recognized that this was his friend's house and was in Hebrew and I don't read Hebrew. Morris must have been a connection, or I wouldn't have even had the image. On the other hand, he didn't know anything about it at all. But he was able to verify it for us. It looks like it was some kind of precognitive event, but it was very clear. It was clear enough that I was willing to describe it to my boss, at the risk of having him think I'm crazy. But he was able to verify it the next day. Even as I describe it now, I feel shocked that I could describe a written document so readily, together with all the other circumstances. That would have been 1954. I was 22 years old, just out of graduate school. It was my first job—In 1954 I was just out of college. This was in 1956 and I was twenty-two. That would have been my first high quality precognition or remote viewing kind of thing.

Mishlove: Just about twenty years before you began your work as a parapsychology researcher.

Targ: That's right. I worked for three years in the field of lasers before there were any lasers because I was working at the Sperry Gyroscope Company. I had an idea that you could see into a plasma, which is the heart of a fusion-generating system, and that you could use microwaves to penetrate that plasma, which turned out to be correct. I got the job at Sperry building high-power microwave devices. One of the things that I built contained a beam of electrons. As I was the engineer, I got permission to add another appendage to this experimental tube to slow down the electrons, and a suitable person could then push that electron beam from one side to the other because it was all in a vacuum with plates on both sides.

Mishlove: Using—do you mean the body?

Targ: Using your mind to move the electrons while holding yourself still.

Mishlove: In other words, psychokinesis.

Targ: Psychokinesis. This was my first rather esoteric ESP experiment, moving a cloud of electrons in a vacuum tube. I rebuilt the system a decade later at Sylvania when I moved to California. The experiment was in Edgar Mitchell's first anthology, *Psychic Exploration,* that he wrote after he returned from space. It was published by my father.

Mishlove: Who was the editor-in-chief of Putnam's at the time.

Targ: Yes. This was a convincing experiment. I published the graphs looking like this: here's our control, and here's our control, and here a guy is thinking about it, and he pushes the electrons all to one side. It looked like a physics experiment.

Mishlove: So a pretty convincing demonstration of psychokinesis. At this point, you're just a few years out of graduate school.

Targ: I'm 22 years old. I'm a kid, but I've got the tools.

Mishlove: Were you the one demonstrating the psychokinesis?

Targ: No. I had another person. I make no claim for psychokinetic ability; though I can do other things, I can't do that as far as I know. I had become friends with Eileen Garrett, who was a famous New York medium at that time.

Mishlove: Who founded the Parapsychology Foundation.

Targ: I happened to meet her because my father had published her autobiography. Eileen Garrett was very interested in a physicist who was pursuing psychic stuff. I had read this monograph called *Mind, Matter, and Gravitation* that Eileen Garrett published about Anton Forwald's dice-throwing machine. Forwald had built an inclined plane where dice would tumble down onto a table. He was not trying to get particular numbers, but to push the column of dice to the left or push them to the right. Forwald was an engineer, and he was a careful guy, so he would sit quietly with his hands folded to make the dice go where he wanted.

Mishlove: He called it, as I recall, PK placement.

Targ: It was this PK placement example that made me think it would be easier using electrons. Forwald's article stimulated me to do with electrons what he had done with dice.

After I became friends with her, she asked, "Could you make one of those for me?" I went back to my laboratory, and, together with some technician help, we made an attractive wooden box with a metal chute that would deliver ten dice onto a corrugated tabletop and then onto a green felt landing pad. With the press of a button, the dice would be released through a shutter, and would roll down to the table. People could influence the dice to move to the left or the right. We made it very stable so it wouldn't move when the shutter was opened.

Eileen Garrett and Karlis Osis, who was research director at the Parapsychology Foundation, used that for many years. In fact, her daughter told me that she used to play with it when she was a child. They had it set up as an exhibit at the Parapsychology Foundation.

Mishlove: This was really the beginning of your work developing instruments for testing and measuring and even training ESP ability.

Targ: I was a technically oriented person, and I would work with big things like this. Though I had very bad vision, I could give an impersonation of somebody who could actually see what they're doing. But my glasses are much, much better now than they were 40 years ago. I have a much higher index of refraction glasses.

Mishlove: But in fact, you're legally blind.

Targ: Well, I'm no longer legally blind. I was riding my motorcycle for many years legally blind. But my new glasses moved me out of that category. It's still bad.

Mishlove: But for most of your life, I gather, you were legally blind.

Targ: That's right.

Mishlove: So here you are, a legally blind physicist doing ESP research.

Targ: When I moved to California, I went to a lecture at Stanford University where Professor Jeffrey Smith was talking about research in parapsychology. He was a very gentle professor of religion, and people were picking on and heckling him during the lecture. He was lecturing about stuff that I knew quite a lot more about than he did, and I helped him from the audience. After his lecture, I said, "Why don't we create a parapsychology group for interested people?" He thought that would be a good idea. He was already working with Charlie Tart, who was a post-doctoral student, and Arthur Hastings, who was a professor there. We formed this little group with Jeffrey Smith, a distinguished professor, Charlie Tart, Arthur Hastings, and me, called the Parapsychology Research Group.

Mishlove: I later became involved with it myself for many years. In the Bay Area of California, it was the premier gathering place for people seriously interested in parapsychology.

Targ: Out of that, I met a young electronic engineer genius named David Hurt. I had the idea for an ESP teaching machine to help people develop their psychic skills. David built a four-choice trainer for me. The person could press one of four buttons, red, blue, yellow, or green before the machine would light up the color.

Mishlove: That are selected at random by the machine.

Targ: That's right. And it had a pass button, so it was not a forced choice.

Mishlove: You had the option to pass if you didn't feel confident.

Targ: We found that by offering feedback, reinforcement, and a pass option, people could get a greater than chance number correct.
   I would not have gone into remote viewing and psychic stuff as a profession if I had not had convincing psychic experiences as a child. I knew this when I was bailing out of my very successful laser program; I would have something to go into that would probably work. When I started the Stargate program at SRI, I was pretty confident we would be able to do something psychic and something successful.

Mishlove: I gather, by now, we're sort of up to, what, the 1960s or so.

Mishlove: Russell, what a fascinating adventure this has been. We're going to do more interviews. I know we've hardly scratched the surface. Thank you so much for being with me.

Targ: Thank you. I'm very happy for the opportunity.

2

Early Years of Psi Research at SRI International

Recorded on March 2, 2017

Jeffrey Mishlove: Today we're going to look at the early years of the remote viewing and ESP research program at SRI International, a military-industrial think tank located in Menlo Park, California. With me is one of the founders of that program, Russell Targ. Russell is a dear and longtime friend.

Russell Targ: Thank you very much.

Mishlove: It's a pleasure to be with you. In an earlier interview, as we were talking about your childhood and your interest as a student in ESP research, we talked about the fact that you had developed—with David Hurt, when you were in California—an ESP teaching machine. In a way, this teaching machine is what led to the development of the program at SRI, isn't it?

Targ: I had an interesting concatenation of experiences. When I was still working with lasers, I was interested in starting an ESP program somewhere. I had an opportunity once to go to the CIA and met Kit Green and was able to tell him about my interest in doing that. That would have been in early 1972. Through a strange collection of events, I had a chance to pitch my idea to Wernher von Braun and the administrator of NASA. If you're interested in coincidences, this is one of the remarkable groups of coincidences I experienced.

So, I'm interested in starting a program. A friend of mine was teaching at Esalen, Jean Millay, whom you probably know. Jean had built a brainwave synchronizer. Tim Scully built a synchronizer for her so that two people could be connected each to their own brainwave machine detectors and then the two machines were connected. The people lying adjacent to one another could get feedback when their two alphas were synchronized and in phase. It was a very unusual thing to want to do. I had done it with Jean and the effect is very strong. That is, when you bring the two signals in phase you feel a very strong connection with that person. Not sexual necessarily, but just a feeling of oneness and non-separation, like a physical oneness; a very powerful surprising effect. She had her brainwave synchronizer at Esalen Institute in Big Sur. She invited me to come with her to show off my ESP teaching machine: it's a four-choice biofeedback device that helps you become aware when you're doing something psychic. So that was my first trip to Esalen in April 1972, before the SRI program.

Jean was doing her thing. I was talking about American and Soviet research in parapsychology and demonstrating my ESP game, *Fortress Trial*. I met Mike Murphy who was the owner and factotum at Esalen. He ran the thing. He owned the property, and he was the inspiring feeling behind Esalen. I had not been there before. I didn't know Mike. But we all had a very nice weekend. The following Monday I got a call from Mike Murphy. He said, "I'm sick as a dog. I've got a lecture to give at Grace Cathedral tomorrow night on Soviet work. I've been in Russia. But I liked your talk on Soviet-American research. Could you go to Grace Cathedral and just give your talk for me?" I thought, Mike's a nice fellow, I've never been to Grace Cathedral. I could do that, no problem.

So on Tuesday I went to Grace Cathedral, a big packed house, a big church sanctuary. I'm standing up by the altar and I give my talk. People seemed very happy with what I was talking about; very interested. At the end of my talk, a businessman walks up to me and says, "Very interesting talk. My name is Art Reetz. I am the new project administrator, that is the administrator of new projects at NASA. I'm having a conference on speculative technology in the first week of May. Would you like to come to Saint Simons Island and tell a hundred or so scientists who are interested in new physics, new ideas; tell them what you're doing with ESP." I said, "Sure, I could do that. Will you send me a ticket?" He said, "I can do that. We'd be happy to have you come."

This was a totally strange occurrence. I didn't know Art Reetz. I didn't know anything about the conference. He didn't know anything about my lecture. He was just at a NASA conference. He was walking down the street in front of Grace Cathedral and saw that somebody was lecturing on Soviet-American ESP research. He had an hour to kill so he just walked in to see me. Total coincidence. I went to the conference and I, of course, brought my little ESP teaching machine with me because I'm still interested in starting a program. And whom should I meet but Wernher von Braun, father of American rockets. I chatted with him.

Like so many high-level people, he is not going to admit that he's psychic, but everybody has a psychic grandmother. Von Braun told me about his grandmother who always knew when something strange was going to happen; usually something bad. He did super well with my ESP game. When you get a hit, that is, when you press the button corresponding to what the machine will choose on that instance, it rings a bell. Von Braun kept ringing the bell, ringing the bell, drew a crowd. I told him I'm interested in using this gadget to help astronauts become psychic so they can become aware of problems on their spacecraft.

The ESP Training Machine used by Wernher von Braun

Now, if that sounds crazy to you, I recognize that. Isaac Asimov created a very intuitive semanticist, Salvor Hardin, who had recipes for an acute life. One of them: *Nothing has to be true; a thing just has to sound true.* Another: *A lie that you don't believe can never succeed.* He had a whole group of those things. I could tell von Braun, I'm interested in helping astronauts psychically to become in touch with their spacecraft, and if I believe that for some reason, he will believe that. And that's what happened. He took me to this big crowd to meet James Fletcher, who is the big boss, the administrator of NASA. Von Braun said, "Targ here has built lasers for us at Redstone Arsenal. I know what he does, and he now has this ESP gadget, and he wants to teach people what it feels like, if they're psychic. He wants $80,000 from NASA to do a program." Fletcher said, "If he's got a place to do that, we might be able to help him."

Now, it just happened, before I went to Saint Simons Island, Hal Puthoff was a physicist at SRI, a graduate from Stanford who was giving a lecture at Stanford on Soviet-American research and parapsychology. I had to go and hear him to find out what the competition is doing. It turned out he's also a laser guy. He'd written a book on non-linear optics and was doing laser stuff at SRI, not ESP at all, but he's very interested in psychic stuff. So, I said to Hal, "I'm going to this NASA conference next week. If I can get some money, would you support my joining SRI to create a program?" He said, "That sounds like a perfectly reasonable thing to do." Because at SRI if you have a reasonable program and money—it's like a farmer's market—you can bring your wagon in and do your thing if you've got money to do it. I told Jim Fletcher, "I believe that I can do this at SRI."

At that moment, as we were standing talking, Edgar Mitchell came walking by. He had just come back from a venture in space, walking on the moon, doing an ESP experiment. He overheard what we were talking about, and he said, "I might be able to help you. I'm working with Willis Harmon at SRI on a new project and starting my new institute, Institute of Noetic Sciences. I could introduce you at SRI." So, with my new friend Art Reetz, the program manager, and Edgar Mitchell, we were able to go to Charlie Anderson, president of SRI. We had a meeting with Edgar Mitchell, Art Reetz, Hal Puthoff, and the president of SRI where I said, "I'm about to get $80,000 from NASA. Will you accept it? And P.S., hire me to do the program." We had this concatenation of a dozen unrelated things that led to Charlie Anderson saying yes, you can do the program at SRI. Those were the entire steps necessary to start the Stargate project at SRI. If Mitchell hadn't been there, if Art Reetz hadn't stumbled into my lecture, etc., there would have been no program because there would have been no money.

This led me to become very interested in the whole idea of coincidence. As you know, both Carl Jung and Wolfgang Pauli were very interested. The two of them wrote a book called *The Interpretation of Nature and the Psyche,* by Carl Jung and Wolfgang Pauli: Carl Jung, the great psychiatrist, and Pauli, the Nobel Prize winning physicist. What Pauli believed eventually is what he called—his Nobel Prize was for the exclusion principle, but from working with Carl Jung he developed—what he calls statistical causality, which says that things occur in a kind of acausal way. Pauli knew that he had a bad reputation.

I don't know if you know that Pauli was a great physicist in Germany, but whenever he would come to town to visit somebody, their experiment would fail. He was a non-experimentally conducive person. You could be doing an experiment and suddenly the whole thing would fail and screw up. Somebody would say, Pauli must be coming to see us. He was aware that something about his thought processes, or his being, somehow interfered with the causality of ordinary physics. It greatly interested him. He wasn't alone. Not only Pauli but David Bohm talked about quantum interconnectedness, the extent to which the things in the universe are connected to one another. Einstein was worried about spooky connection at a distance being a manifestation of non-local physics in addition to non-local consciousness. There are a lot of Nobel Prize winning scientists, physicists, who are aware that there is something the matter with our causality. Today, physicists believe that if you don't understand causality, you don't understand anything.

It interests me that you have this whole group of very famous physicists, all of whom were worried about the nature of causality, i.e., things that occur that are not very probable. I once had an occurrence like that where—I have a radio on my desk here and I just sometimes listen to classical music from the local music station at a university. I was listening to music one day when I called a friend of mine who was a physicist in Philadelphia who was sick. He was dying of cancer. I frequently chatted with him; we had a good time talking to one another. He said, "What are you listening to?" I said, "I think they are playing a piano reduction of the Beethoven Fifth Symphony." Now, most people don't even know what that would be. That's the case where somebody has taken a Beethoven symphony and rewritten it for the piano. I knew what that was because I had musical friends. He said, "I can't believe that that's what you're listening to because I'm sitting here at the piano and I'm beginning to practice stuff that I played in college. On the piano here is the piano reduction of the Beethoven Fifth Symphony, which I'm playing at the time you called me. What do you think of that?"

Mishlove: You have some interesting cases here. In Pauli's case, equipment breaks down around him. But in your case, it seems as if things come together, like the whole parapsychology research program at SRI, which had an enormous, I would even call it revolutionary, influence on our culture.

Targ: I think that's true. As I wrote down the group of things, it's an amazing collection of unrelated—If Mike Murphy hadn't gotten sick, I wouldn't have gone to Grace Cathedral. If Art Reetz didn't happen to walk down the street past that church, we wouldn't have gone to that conference. If Wernher von Braun didn't get super good scores with my ESP game, he wouldn't have taken me to Jim Fletcher. A dozen different things had to happen, most of them quite improbable, for that program. It's as though the Stargate project was foredestined. It was like the universe was continuing to give us a push to make the program get started.

People often ask me, "You guys had a very easy time. Everybody gives you money, you publish your papers in *Nature* and the *Proceedings of the IEEE*, you got a couple of million dollars a year. How did you do that?" The answer is, "We have no idea." Hal and I were known physicists. We both had successful careers in laser physics, so we could at least get in the door. Then we worked with Pat Price, a highly psychic guy, who knew what he was doing and was successful. The CIA liked us.

Mishlove: They were taking a big risk because parapsychology in general has always been controversial. There were people who called themselves skeptics, who were really scoffers, [who] could be very, very nasty.

Targ: Hal and I had no credentials for doing ESP research. I was very well known as a laser physicist. Hal, with a PhD from Stanford, wrote a book on quantum electronics, so we had already established our credentials as people who were able to do something technical. So, if a person is thinking of a career in parapsychology, I would encourage them to do some other thing first that your sponsors can recognize.

Mishlove: The opposite of what I did.

Targ: That's right. What I observed as a physics student at Queens College in Columbia is that there's basically no money for parapsychology, and I think that has not changed. But if you're an expert in something else, you can attract money because people recognize that you're able to get difficult things done.

Mishlove: Otherwise, you need to be, largely, an entrepreneurial spirit, which I suppose would characterize my career more.

Targ: Well, you made a lot of contributions as well.

Mishlove: I did, but I never received funding from NASA. I never had a position at a major military industrial think tank or a major college or university. Because of the path I chose, those things were pretty much out of the question, especially, frankly, Russell, after you introduced me to the PK man. But that's another story.

Targ: People often want to know, if I made a big sacrifice to go into parapsychology after being a laser pioneer. I said, "Not at all! I gave myself a 20% pay raise to go from Sylvania to SRI." Because, I explained to SRI, it was a much more difficult field than laser work. Hal and I didn't know what was going to happen; whether we were going to destroy our careers. I was bringing in a little money, but we didn't know at the time that it would be a $20 million, twenty-year program. So, we had a very successful opportunity to move forward in the psychic arena.

Mishlove: You were fortunate in those early years to be able to work with some very talented individuals.

Targ: That's true. Before we stop discussing this little ESP game, I want to tell you that it is still alive. Fifty years later, you can now have your own ESP teaching machine as an application for your cell phone. It's called ESP Trainer, and it's free from the App Store.

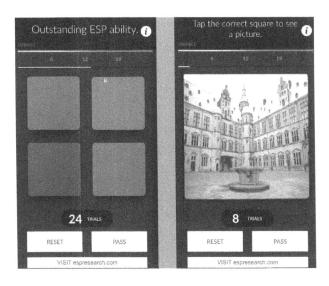

Modern ESP Trainer Designed by Russell Targ.

Mishlove: It's your gift to the world.

Targ: It's my gift. A Buddhist would not charge for the dharma.

Mishlove: Well, I should say it's one of your many gifts, Russell, because I know you have given of yourself freely for decades.

Targ: I've done my best. It's been a very interesting opportunity. I met a lot of people.

Mishlove: Indeed, you did. You've met some extraordinary people along the way, not just in the parapsychological arena, but in other social circumstances. Even your famous brother-in-law, Bobby Fisher, perhaps the greatest chess player who ever lived.

Targ: I think that that's true.

Mishlove: To go back to the situation at SRI, you and Hal Puthoff have now established a program. The head of SRI has given it its blessing. You've gotten a grant from NASA to work on the ESP teaching machine. Then, I gather, as word spread that this project had been established, other talented people came along.

Targ: Hal was in touch with Ingo Swann, who was a New York artist and had already done significant psychic things like out-of-body experiments with Eileen Garrett and Karlis Osis. An out-of-body experiment is one that you're not only describing a distant location or building, but you seem to go there and wander around the halls. We can talk about that later.

Ingo is with us, and Hal and I, in our physicist way, would ask him, "Can you describe what's in the box, or what's in the envelope, or what's in the next room?" Swiftly, Ingo became unhappy with that limitation. He said, "This remote viewing allows you to focus your attention anywhere on the planet. I can see anything in the universe, and what you're having me do is a trivialization of my ability. I'm going to go home and resume painting." I said, "Well, what do you want to do?" He said, "Why don't you have somebody hide in the Bay Area, and I'll describe where they are." So, Ingo is really the father of remote viewing as we did it for the next couple of decades.

Mishlove: I suppose it's worth mentioning that Hal Puthoff and Ingo Swann were both Scientologists, and I imagine that their Scientology training inclined them toward this sort of thing.

Targ: It's true, Hal and Ingo were Scientologists, but I and many, many other people who worked with us were not Scientologists. Scientology might be a permission-giving device, but it's not necessary. From my point of view, becoming a Scientologist is an unnecessarily high price to pay to develop psychic abilities.

Mishlove: Did Ingo or Hal discuss any of that at the time?

Targ: I was quite familiar with their protocol. Hal was very forthcoming with what it was all about and what it required, but I was not having any of it. I said, "Let's just do what we're doing. It seems to be working fine."

Mishlove: Did Ingo acquire his remote-viewing abilities because of that background?

Targ: I think Ingo was a lifetime, genetic, childhood psychic. I think most of these prodigious psychics were early showers.

Ingo is the one who brought us the idea of analytical overlay as a source of noise. He was cognizant of the problems of signal-to-noise ratio, whereas the job of the psychic is to separate the mental noise from the psychic signal. The job of the interviewer [was] to help keep that happening. A viewer knows that he's there to give an answer, but it's not like a test [subject] that is struggling to figure out what the answer is. That is not the way to do it. You must relax and let the answer come to you. The interviewer has the job of creating a peaceful environment. I instruct the viewer not to tell me where Joe is hiding. Just to tell me about the surprising images that come into your awareness regarding where Joe is now. Since I don't know anything, I can do whatever I want to do to try and help you do that.

Another person I did a very similar thing with was Jeffrey Mishlove.

Mishlove: Oh, I know him.

Targ: Can I tell that story?

Mishlove: Yes, indeed.

Targ: This is another demonstration of my non-psychic ESP. You had just received your PhD, I think, in 1980.

Mishlove: This was in 1976, Russell. I was still a graduate student.

Targ: All right. But you were an aspiring ESP researcher.

Mishlove: Yes.

Targ: You came to the lab and said, "Russ, you've been publishing this psychic stuff in *Nature* magazine; makes it seem like it's probably true. Can you show me how it works?"

We sat down, and Elizabeth Rauscher—who is another physicist— she went to hide somewhere along with Hal Puthoff. And I said, "Jeffrey, here we are. What do you see regarding Elizabeth?" You said, "It looks to me like Macy's department store." In my mind, that answer did not sound like remote viewing. It sounded like naming or guessing. I rudely said, "Don't tell me about Macy's. Let's take a break. Tell me what you're experiencing." You said, "Well, I see a bunch of wire hangers, one in front of the other, a whole row of wire hangers on some horizontal post. That's why I said Macy's." I said, "Well, that's a very interesting description. Could you draw that?"

"The magic word", I said, "is, what are you *experiencing* that makes you think of Macy's?" You then described the coat hangers and the wires and so forth. You made a splendid description of the pedestrian overpass.

It turned out that Elizabeth was standing at a pedestrian overpass over Bayshore Freeway, and where Hal was standing, if you looked where he was standing, what you saw is a bunch of triangular pieces of wire forming the pedestrian overpass, amazingly like what you had drawn.

Mishlove: Yes, you could have put my drawing right over the photograph. It was practically a perfect match. But I didn't consciously perceive that. I still was imagining a rack of clothing.

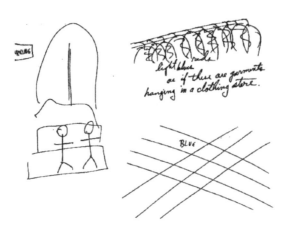

Drawings made by Jeffrey Mishlove during his first remote viewing trial at SRI International in February 1976.

Pedestrian overpass target for Mishlove's remote viewing trial.

Targ: That's right. It's the job of the interviewer, even though I don't know the answer, of course, to help you to separate your desire to guess and to name it. The desire to name the target is what makes it very, very hard for certain kinds of ESP experiments to work.

Mishlove: You worked with Ingo Swann. You worked with Joe McMoneagle. You worked with Hella Hammid and Pat Price. All of these people were some of the top remote viewers in history. Somebody might well say, you were just lucky in getting talented people to work with you. The interesting thing to me is, from that group, you originally selected Hella Hammid to be a control subject, because you had no reason to think she had any remote viewing talent.

Targ: That's right. It's a very important outcome from our decade. We started with Pat Price, who was a lifetime experienced psychic and [who] did phenomenally accurate descriptions and drawings of distant places. It was just very amazing. Day after day, he would make these accurate drawings. Ingo Swann, of course, taught us how to do that. Then Ken Kress, who was our contract monitor, said, "I want to see somebody who's not a lifetime psychic. Can you find somebody who's never done this before?" I invited Hella to come and work with us. She was a professional photographer, an old friend of the family, woman of the world, and always willing to try something new. She thought it was very amusing to be paid for being a psychic for the CIA. It was a whole new departure for her.

On our very first time, she was wearing her remote viewing socks with little eyeballs crocheted onto the toes, because she took this all very seriously. She said, "Okay, what do I do now, Russ? I'm just lying here.

What should I do?" I told her to describe her experience, what comes into your mind that's new and unusual. She described those famous squares within squares of a pedestrian overpass. That was her very first trial and it was an excellent drawing. The kind that is the archetype of a good remote viewing. I was able to help her do that through a series of steps. She eventually caught on quite well and needed hardly any guidance at all.

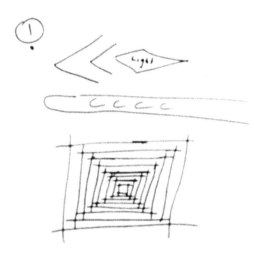

Hella Hammid's first remote viewing. Her drawings. The remote viewing target happened to be the very same highway overpass as in the Mishlove trial.

What's interesting is that, in her nine trials, her descriptions were so accurate that she was able to achieve overall significance ten times greater than the most psychic man in the world. Hella's results were significant at one in a million. Pat Price was one in one hundred thousand. They're both highly significant, remarkable results. Hella was much more parsimonious in her descriptions. She often would say very, very little, but what she said was almost always correct. Where sometimes Pat would go off on a wild goose chase and significantly miss. We became confident, then, because of Hella's very good result, that remote viewing may not be as unique as we thought.

Ingo Swann and Hella Hammid.

Mishlove: At the same time, though, I understand Ingo Swann and your partner Hal Puthoff did develop a training program.

Targ: Yes, I'm not sure that Hal was involved. Ingo and I quarreled over that. Ingo's training program involved him sitting with a viewer of the day. Ingo would have a picture and he would try and guide the viewer to get images that corresponded to what he would see later. However, Ingo knew the answer. We considered that extremely bad protocol for several reasons. First, what you're doing is teaching the person to read Ingo's mind. So, he's going to look and see what kind of images he gets from Ingo by mental telepathy. We think there is such a thing. You're also teaching him to look into his future and very often a viewer will not get feedback. So, one of the important things we know is, although feedback is helpful when you're first learning, it's not essential to an experienced remote viewer. They don't need feedback. So, the fact that Ingo is sitting in front of a picture, face down presumably, and trying to guide the viewer to experience that picture, I thought that was a terrible protocol. I would never do that. It's not necessary. I felt it to be sort of an anti-training procedure.

About that time, we were doing experiments for the CIA, who were interested in our work, and Pat Price [1918-1975], who was another Scientologist, probably heard about it over the grapevine and said, "I've been doing that all my life as a police commissioner. I'd quiet my mind and describe where the crook was hiding, and we'd go and pick him up."

When Price came to work with us, the CIA was very interested in remote viewing, and they said, "You guys are wasting your time playing psychic hide-and-go-seek in the Bay Area." What we had been doing until then is the experiment that Ingo Swann described. Hal would usually go hide with another SRI manager, because we always had oversight in these experiments. [Neither] Hal nor I could never do an experiment without oversight from our watchdog committee.

They would randomly choose one of sixty locations that I knew nothing about and go hide there for half an hour. I would sit with Price initially and say, "Can you describe where Hal and Joe are located now?" Price would say that he saw boat dock or a swimming pool or a church or whatever it was. When Hal and Joe came back, we would all go visit the place. Price seemed to be doing very well. All these things are done in an electrically shielded room.

Mishlove: So, no possibility of radio communication.

Targ: That's right. I was with Price, Hal and our contract monitor from the CIA, Kit Green, who was the branch chief of the life science division, a highly intelligent physician and CIA agent. Hal and Kit Green went to hide somewhere as I'm sitting with Price and I said, "They've gone to their target today; what are your impressions?" He said, "You know, I really don't see anything, nothing comes into view." In my continuing guise of trying to be a helpful interviewer, I said, "Hal's taking his little green car, why don't you just follow it out of the parking lot and see where they're going?" He said, "Oh, I can do that. They're heading south on Middlefield Road."

He drew a square pool of water and a round pool of water, and a little building, and said: "It looks like a water purification plant, and I see two big water tanks." I said, "That's a very interesting drawing." Half an hour later, Hal and Kit came back. They had gone to Rinconada swimming pool, which had a 100-foot diameter round pool and a rectangular pool, 60 by 80 feet, perfectly matching what Price drew, but there are no water tanks. My story was that Price described his place excellently and made up the water tanks from his memory and imagination.

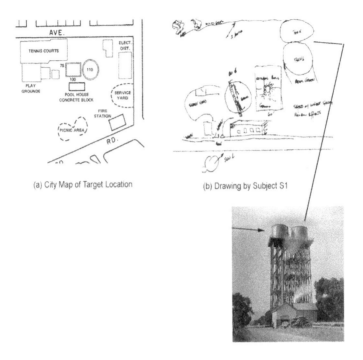

(a) City Map of Target Location   (b) Drawing by Subject S1

Pat Price's sketch of the target location, Rinconada Park; the City map of the target location, Rinconada Park, and the original photo of the Rinconada water purification plant, showing two large towers.

Mishlove: Which often happens in remote viewing.

Targ: Ten years later, on the 100th anniversary of the city of Palo Alto, we all got a picture book. Rinconada used to be a water purification plant. It had the two water tanks that Price drew that were there a hundred years ago, and they would have been the biggest thing in Palo Alto.

Mishlove: So unbeknownst to him, he was doing retrocognition.

Targ: He was looking ...

Mishlove: Backwards in time.

Targ: That's right. He was looking five miles down Middlefield Road and a hundred years into the past.

Mishlove: Or at least some kind of residue impression was still there from those towers that had been there in the past and had been, I presume, taken down long, long ago.

Targ: That's right. We did nine trials like that with Pat Price and each time he would try to describe where Hal was hiding. An analyst would try to match up all nine of Price's transcripts against the nine traveling orders for the destinations. They would stand at Rinconada Park and say, "Which of these nine transcripts is the best match?"

They got seven out of nine first place matches, which is to say, if Hal were kidnapped nine days in a row, Pat Price would have found him the first place he looked seven out of nine times. That's significant with odds of 1:100,000. It was really a remarkable result. In fact, when I presented that data at the Parapsychology Conference in 1975 in Santa Barbara, people thought we were lying because these results were stronger than people had ever seen in ESP experiments.

Target Location	Distance (km)	Rank of Associated Transcript
Hoover Tower, Stanford	3.4	1
Baylands Nature Preserve, Palo Alto	6.4	1
Radio telescope, Portola Valley	6.4	1
Marina, Redwood City	6.8	1
Bridge toll plaza, Fremont	14.5	6
Drive-in theater, Palo Alto	5.1	1
Arts and Crafts Plaza, Menlo Park	1.9	1
Catholic Church, Portola Valley	8.5	3
Swimming pool complex, Palo Alto	3.4	1
Total sum of ranks		16 $(p = 2.9 \times 10^{-5})$

Results of initial remote viewing tests with Pat Price.
7 out of 9 first place hits.

Mishlove: At that time, people were doing mostly the forced choice kinds of experiments.

Targ: That's right. Guessing locations in a naturalistic setting like this where your friend is hiding somewhere is infinitely easier than card guessing, because you've got the mental noise of your knowledge of the possible cards. Whether it's a diamond, heart, spade, or club, you've got those burned into your memory. If I tell you I'm looking at a card, it's very hard to separate the diaphanous image brought to you by ESP from your lifelong memory of playing cards.

Mishlove: I know your critics at that point in time began to pounce all over this research to tear it apart and find something wrong. I think they looked at, for example, subtle cues that might have helped the judges in their matching process.

Targ: They can find subtle cues, but when the person draws a map of Rinconada Park that essentially lays over the map that's in the city plan, that can't be your lucky day.

Mishlove: You became very gifted as what we call "the monitor."

Targ: That's right, the interviewer. I was with Hella and each day we would ask her to describe where Hal or usually Hal and a contract monitor were hiding. We did nine trials with her because the CIA wanted to know how a control subject would do compared with the great psychic policeman. Hella did superior to the psychic policeman in her trials; whereas Price did wonderfully well at odds of 1:100,000, Hella was significant with odds of 1:1,000,000.

Mishlove: It would lead one to think, I suppose, since she said she had no psychic ability, that there must be some sensory leakage going on somewhere.

Targ: She wouldn't say that she had no psychic ability. She said she had never done anything like this before.

Mishlove: Pretty close.

Targ: If you'd asked her, "Do you think you're intuitive?" She would have probably said yes.

Mishlove: Let me ask you this question, Russell. What was your expectation at the time? Did you think she would have had a null result?

Targ: No, I expected her to do very well. I was betting my career that all people have psychic abilities, and people can learn to do it. I had a previous decade using the ESP teaching machine. I had an expectation that psychic ability is available. I bet on that because I had had psychic abilities as a young person. The CIA was very amazed that Hella did so well, and they subsequently sent us some other people to see how their agents would do, and to observe our programs. They sent us two agents, both of whom did excellently in this protocol.

Mishlove: With regard to the other talented people, you worked with—Ingo Swann, Hella Hammid, Joe McMoneagle, and I'm sure there are a few others who weren't involved at the level that Pat Price was with the CIA—they've all managed to live out their lives without any sort of hint of foul play. I guess maybe the lesson is, you must be careful whom you're working with.

Targ: That's right. Hella was in no danger. She lived to be 72. She unfortunately died of cancer. Looking back, I now think that 72 is young. Ingo Swann was not really working for the CIA, in the way that Price was. I think, if you get in bed with the CIA and become an operative and are then read into a lot of top secret, funny business the CIA is doing, you really put yourself in jeopardy, in my opinion. I don't think that Hella considered herself in danger. Nor do I think she was ever in any danger.

Targ: It was a remarkable decade. We had made this amazing calculation, working with Hella Hammid, the psychic photographer, control subject, and my old friend. We designed an experiment with the fewest number of trials [in which] we could have a statistically significant outcome if she got all of them correct. No rational scientist would ever design an experiment to choose the power of the experiment, and the number of trials to do, assuming everything worked perfectly without errors.

Mishlove: Certainly not in the behavioral sciences.

Targ: If we were to do four experiments and all of them were first place matches, the statistics of that would be one in four factorials, or about 0.02, which would be across the magical 0.05 barrier. So we signed up to do four precognitive experiments with Hella.

Mishlove: They all had to be first place hits.

Targ: I would sit down with Hella in our shielded room at 9 o'clock, and say, "Around 11 o'clock, Hal will be somewhere. Right now, he hasn't arrived at SRI yet, but sometime this morning he will arrive, go to the safe, be handed traveling instructions, and go someplace. I'd like you to describe where Hal will be at 11 o'clock, and where you and I will be at 12." She did four remote views, and all four were first place matched. As crystal clear as though she was looking out of her psychic window, she described a swing set at a playground, a manicured garden, which happened to be Stanford Hospital, a muddy square in the water, which was low tide at the Baylands, and Palo Alto City Hall.

Mishlove: You make it sound easy, and I know that for people who attempt to replicate this work, it's usually not that easy.

Mishlove: You, in effect, introduced them to the protocol.

Targ: That's right. We had a woman mechanical engineer, Ph.D., from the CIA named Francine, who said, "I've seen what you're doing now with my partner here. I want to sit in the room by myself. You guys go hide somewhere." She made a spectacularly accurate drawing of a randomly chosen target. The manager gave us traveling orders from the safe. We got in the car and read what they said: "Go to this merry-go-round in Rinconada Park." Francine drew a cupola with a six-sided thing on top of a building that looked just like the merry-go-round.

Mishlove: This might be an example of somebody whom you didn't have ongoing interaction with. She was a CIA agent.

Targ: She showed up for a week and then left.

Mishlove: For all we know, people like her, who have been through SRI or some of the other official remote viewing projects, went back to their agencies and may have developed programs of their own that were not visible to the parapsychologists.

Targ: We know that they did do that. Pat Price left SRI and went to work for the CIA. He worked with the two agents who were sent to us. The CIA had their own little community of remote viewers.

Mishlove: It's theoretically possible then that, even though the SRI program shut down and the subsequent programs that are publicly known to people are no longer in operation, there may have been parallel programs of which we're not aware.

Targ: To this day. I wouldn't be surprised.

Mishlove: Well, that's an interesting observation. I know eventually you contributed to the remote viewing program, as a viewer yourself, but prior to then, had you ever tested your psychic abilities?

Targ: I was never really tested in my lifetime. I took part in one remote viewing experiment at SRI in our 10 years. We had great psychics like Hella Hammid, Ingo Swann, Pat Price, Joe McMoneagle: four people who are outstanding premier remote viewers. They were able to quiet their minds and see what's going on in the distance or see what's going on in the future. Then they would describe and draw what's at the distant location. They did that highly significantly; all of them were people who could do experiments at odds of one in a million. But this was not me. The experiment you're talking about was a long-distance series. Pat Price and I would sit in our little shielded room. Pat would describe where in South America Hal Puthoff was traveling, on a vacation. Hal was gone for ten days. We realized this would be an outstanding time to do a controlled experiment. We weren't looking for American hostages or Russian bomb tests; this was under our control. Hal knew where he would be, and, of course, Pat Price and I in California had no idea where he was traveling. Each day, Pat would say, "I see a harbor," or "I see a church," or "I see a volcano," or "I see a marketplace." On day five, Price didn't show up. I'm sitting in my little room. So in the spirit of the show must go on, I said, "I will describe what I see."

What I saw was a small airport on an island with sand and grass on the left, an airport building on the right, and an ocean at the end of the runway. I drew that. That's the only remote viewing I ever did for the program. It turned out to be a surprisingly accurate picture, so that somebody could fly by and take a picture of the airport. It greatly resembles what I drew.

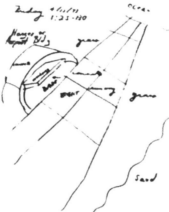

Sketch by Russell Targ of from his first remote viewing experience, indicating an airport terminal, with a runway near the ocean, and photo of the Airport, San Andreas Colombia.
The target was the airport in San Andreas, Colombia.

Mishlove: In fact, I would say that particular drawing and transcript would rank up there with the McMoneagle, Pat Price, Hella Hammid and Ingo Swann examples.

Targ: Yes, it does. The interesting thing is [that] it shows that remote viewing is so easy; even a scientist can do it. It doesn't require metaphysical training.

Mishlove: A direct hit.

Targ: Turned out to be a direct hit. The good news from this is not that I'm psychic, but that remote viewing is so easy that even a scientist can do it.

Mishlove: We often think of scientists as being very obtuse. But I think, in your case, you have such an intense focus on what you do, and, on top of that, an extraordinary sense of confidence that this is doable. It's contagious, and people who work with you seem to pick that up.

Targ: I think that's right. For example, there's Bob Rosenthal's experimenter effect. The experimenter gets what he wants from his experiment and contrives the experiment so that it works.

Mishlove: You're probably one of the top two or three most successful experimenters in the history of parapsychology.

Targ: I've had a lot of talented people to work with. In our next group were people from the U.S. Army.

Mishlove I'll tell you what, we'll pursue that in yet another interview.

Targ: We'll stand by for the Army. [Laughter]

Mishlove: Yes. Because this is a rare opportunity to have you in the studio and to review this very important history with you. I'm happy to do it in as much detail and depth as we can manage. Russell, thank you so much for being with me.

Targ: Thank you.

3

Military Intelligence Interest in Remote Viewing

Recorded on March 2, 2017

Jeffrey Mishlove: Today we're going to look at remote viewing, what makes it work and how the US Army got involved in the remote viewing research program. With me is the remote viewing pioneer Russell Targ, one of the founders of the remote viewing research program at SRI International.

Russell Targ: Thank you very much, I'm happy to be with you.

Mishlove: It's great to be with you. In previous interviews we've talked about your interest in parapsychology since childhood and how you developed an ESP teaching machine and helped inaugurate the remote viewing research program at SRI International with support from NASA and the CIA. As the program was more and more successful, you found more and more government agencies expressing an interest in it, including the US Army.

Targ: That's right. I can say a word about the CIA; people want to know: "What is a nice guy like you doing working for the CIA?" The deal we made with the CIA is that we would spend half of our time doing research trying to understand the mechanism of psychic abilities, how to make it work better and publish papers in the open literature about our exploits trying to understand psychic ability. We would spend the other half of our time doing operational things for the CIA: looking for missing airplanes, looking for captives, kidnapped people, downed Russian submarines, Soviet weapons factories, Chinese bomb tests, all the kind of things that the CIA would be interested in; and we were successful enough with the operational things.

We found a downed Russian bomber that Jimmy Carter was very interested in, and he even included that in his recent book in a chapter called "Clairvoyance: Where the CIA Team Found a Russian Bomber that Satellite Photography Couldn't Find." Although we're talking about psychic hide-and-go-seek in California where we try and locate and describe where somebody is hiding in the San Francisco Bay area, what paid our rent was finding the downed bomber and the missing submarine.

Mishlove: I think it is interesting that you're doing this work, which is highly controversial, and they're paying for it but they would allow you to speak publicly and publish. In fact, in the early years, you and Hal co-authored a very popular book called *Mind-Reach* that was accessible to thousands and thousands of people about this research.

Targ: We published a paper in *Nature* magazine in England, which is the most prestigious worldwide scientific journal, and then we published a whole summary of our work in the proceedings of the Engineering Society, the IEEE, with a 25-page paper that went all over the world including the Soviet Union describing the details of our work. [See Appendix 1] Of course, there's no missing submarines in that work; that was all our psychic hide-and-seek or sending brainwave images to another person. But the CIA was very open to our publishing the non-operational findings. So, we made a deal with the devil and the devil kept their part of the bargain.

Mishlove: This naturally attracted a lot of public attention that a very prestigious research organization like SRI International had this program going on.

Targ: That's right. This work was quickly replicated at Mundelein College in Chicago and then it was picked up by Professor Robert Jahn at Princeton University who created a whole institute in Princeton to replicate our work, which he did for 20 years. This is not just weird stuff that happened in California. This was replicated in Princeton and Chicago and even in the Soviet Union.

Mishlove: I at that time in the mid-1970s was a graduate student just starting to study parapsychology through an individual major at Berkeley. At that time—we'll talk about it later—you invited me to come visit you at SRI to experience what you were doing, and I did.

Targ: You did very well.

Mishlove: Let's talk now about the interest of the US Army.

Targ: We had done these experiments for the CIA where Hella [Hammid] and Pat Price were able to describe quite accurately where people were hiding, and the Army Intelligence Command obviously decided that this would be a useful ability to train their officers. If you could find out where somebody is kidnapped or a sniper is hiding, all sorts of things that the Army would like to know in the course of being in the field. Can you train an Army Intelligence Officer to develop those psychic abilities?

Hal Puthoff and I—Hal was my colleague at SRI, co-founder of the program—we were invited to Fort Meade, which is an Army base in Maryland, to interview thirty people who are willing to gamble with their career to consider doing psychic exploits with a bunch of people in California. There were thirty people who volunteered to take part in an ESP research and development program, developing their own psychic ability. We interviewed those people and chose six.

Mishlove: The initial thirty, I presume, were selected by a process that the Army had already instituted.

Targ: That's right. The Army chose thirty for us to interview and we talked to each of them, and, in our best psychoanalytic manner, figured out which of these six people would be the best viewers. Of course, Hal and I have no experience in psychology at all. We just chatted with these people and chose six in accordance with our experience working with Ingo Swann and Pat Price and Hella. Each of these soldiers would come out for a week to be with us.

The first person I chose was Joe McMoneagle, who described landing in Vietnam. As he was leaving the troop ship, the aircraft, he saw a yellow passenger plane right in his future, which wasn't there. He knew that having gotten this clear image of the yellow plane that he would safely leave Vietnam. A few months later he was carried out by Air America after an injury and it was a big yellow airplane. That convinced him and it convinced me that he probably had some psychic ability.

Mishlove: He became one of the great remote viewers.

Targ: Yes. Joe McMoneagle is probably the premier American remote viewer today. He got his start with our program. He arrived with his leather jacket and his boots and said, "Okay, what am I supposed to do?" I said, "It's very easy. Hal and your commanding officer Scotty Watt have gone to hide someplace. I have no idea where it is. I don't know anything about the target pool. I don't know where they've gone. But this is really very easy. If you will just quiet your mind, and here's a pencil and paper, and just make a drawing of the surprising elements that show up in your awareness. You're the only one who knows that so you really can't be wrong. I just want you to quiet your mind and make a little sketch of what's interesting and surprising regarding where Hal and Scotty have gone."

Joe made a number of little drawings around the page, and I said, "Well, I see several things here. They're getting ready to come home. Which of these things do you think really pertains to where they are?" He said, "Well, in the middle here we've got a building with tall columns in front, the tall vertical structure, and behind is a lower building. That's what I think the answer is." It turns out they had gone to exactly such a building, Stanford University Art Museum, and Joe had created an almost architecturally accurate drawing of that.

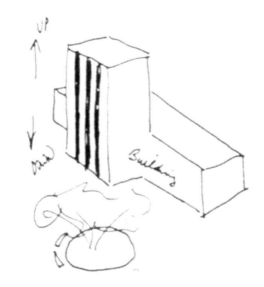

Joe McMoneagle sketch, art museum target.

Stanford University Art Museum.

Mishlove: Both Joe McMoneagle and Pat Price seemed to have this ability to render beautiful drawings.

Targ: That's right. They certainly have. We did six trials with Joe, and in blind matching, five out of those six turned out to be first place matching. I then interviewed five more of the people, one of whom was a woman, and four of those five did independently significant, excellent, remote viewing. Hal and I should be congratulated unless all these people are psychic. But four of our six people were outstanding and went on to honorable careers in remote viewing for the US Army. Joe was given a particularly distinguished award for his lifetime service just for remote viewing, having done 160 applied remote viewings to the intelligence community. He was given an award when he left service.

Mishlove: I believe it was the Legion of Merit award?

Targ: The Legion of Merit award. That's the highest award to a non-serving officer. Of those people, we did thirty-six trials with them. If this was a "lucky day" effect, you would expect each of them to get one of their six first place matches.

Mishlove: In other words, the judges matched them against six possible targets.

Targ: That's right.

Mishlove: The odds of a single hit by chance alone are one in six.

Targ: That's right. You expect six out of the thirty-six to be first place matches, and they got nineteen. It's again a result like one in 100,000 from people who had never done anything like this before. You could say, "Well, how significant is this?" There's another factor besides the probability, one in 100,000 is quite amazing, but we also talked about the effect size, that is, how strong an effect is this? The effect size is the number of standard deviations; that is, how amazing it is, divided by the square root of the number of trials. If you do lots and lots of trials, the thing becomes more significant, but we only did thirty-six trials. The so-called effect size was 0.6. You say, "Well, is that good or bad? What does that mean?" You can compare it with the effect size for the famous experiment that the National Institutes of Health did to determine whether aspirin prevents heart attacks. They did millions of trials with hundreds of thousands of people, and they concluded that the effect is so strong that aspirin prevents heart attacks that you've got to quit the experiment. Their effect size was 0.06.

Mishlove: One-tenth the size.

Targ: That's right. The NIH stopped an experiment because it was so strongly proven, and their effect size was only ten percent of what we had.

Mishlove: In other words, they stopped the experiment because they thought it was unfair to the people in the control group.

Targ: That's right.

Mishlove: That this is such a great effect, everybody should be able to benefit from it right away. Today, I take a baby aspirin every day prescribed by my doctor.

Targ: You could say that the evidence for ESP is ten times stronger than the idea that that aspirin will help you.

Mishlove: Isn't it ironic, Russell, that with all of this good evidence, and especially for you and your very successful career, that there's any controversy at all at this point?

Targ: Well, it's controversial for several reasons. One is that some other people are not able to replicate our work. The other is that we don't have a totally successful explanation for how this works. Our contribution is that we greatly increase the likelihood that the experiment is going to be successful, in that we're able to help the viewer separate the psychic signal from the mental noise.

Mishlove: Which is one of your gifts as an interviewer.

Targ: It's the interviewer's job to pull out of the viewer what he's experiencing without naming it. A source of the mental noise is memory, imagination, and analysis, together with naming and guessing and grasping.

Mishlove: All normal mental habits.

Targ: For example, in our work now for 20 years, we never see a decline effect. Hella Hammid who was with us for a decade, turned in excellent work for her entire decade. She did not decline.

Mishlove: No decline, whereas with the forced choice, card guessing types of experiments, the decline effect became normal.

Targ: That's right. JB Rhine introduced scientific ESP research to the world, and he did that by having people guess cards. The good news is that many people could guess cards correctly over long periods of time. The bad news is that almost all of them eventually declined to chance. That did not wipe out their good results, but it was very disappointing.

Mishlove: It certainly gave the debunkers and scoffers ammunition to use.

Targ: The problem is that if I ask you day after day to tell me what card is coming up, where it's a circle, square, wavy line, or cross, you have those images burned into your subconscious. So I say, "What have I got here?" He says, "Another one of those damn symbols; which one could it be?" It's a very, very difficult task.

Mishlove: It becomes mind-numbing at a certain point.

Targ: One of the effects that Rhine found is this inevitable decline. As compared with remote viewing, where you're guessing realistic outdoor targets, we saw no decline. Joe McMoneagle is still working with physicist Ed May, and Joe has now been doing remote viewing for twenty years, and his work is as excellent as it ever was, probably better. Although people don't get better and better at remote viewing, they get more skillful at separating the psychic signal from the mental noise. That is, the mental noise is memory and imagination and analysis, naming, grasping, and guessing—you learn not to do those things.

Mishlove: Would you say that you trained Joe and the other initial recruits?

Targ: Training is an overstatement. Remote viewing is a natural ability. I basically gave him permission to use an ability he already had. I used to do workshops at Esalen where I would have a couple dozen people for a weekend. I would have them do various, different kinds of tasks. Find the hidden person; describe the object in the box, things like that, to learn the process of separating the signal from the noise. With Joe, he was so ready. He said, "No, no, I've never done anything like this." I said, "Hal has gone somewhere with your colonel. They've gone to hide. Can you describe where he is?" He made several little drawings. I said, "It's coming to the end of the allotted time. Of these drawings, which one do you like best?" He said, "I like this one here," a long, low building in front of a higher building with pillars in front, like piano keys, and a fountain, too. It was really a splendid architectural drawing of the Stanford Art Museum.

Mishlove: As I recall, later, he produced a very complex architectural looking drawing of the Lawrence Livermore Laboratory.

Targ: Yes, he did. Joe was an accomplished architectural artist. He could draw whatever he could see whether it was in front of him or psychically. I had Joe and five other people who claimed to have never done anything like this, certainly no remote viewing, and, of those six people, four of them were outstanding. The whole group together performed at odds of better than a million to one. I did six trials with each of the six people—thirty-six trials—so you would expect six to be in first-place matches, by luck alone.

Mishlove: Because there were six targets in the pool, I assume.
Targ: That's right. We got nineteen first-place matches, which was startlingly accurate. When we presented data like this to the parapsychological conference, people simply thought we were lying. No one had ever seen ESP data at odds of a million to one, with only thirty trials. You typically must do hundreds of thousands of trials to get something at odds of a million to one. Our effect size, or the statistical significance divided by the number of trials—basically the strength of what you're looking at—was much greater than what anybody had seen

before. They couldn't believe that a couple of physicists had invented a way to do ESP. And it worked a hundred times better than anyone had seen in the history of parapsychology.

Mishlove: What you were doing used to be known as free-response clairvoyance. People doing free-response clairvoyance: their tests go back for many, many decades. Why is it that you believe your results were more successful?

Targ: I understand what you're asking me. It's an interesting question. I think it was successful because—I'm making this up now—I think we were the first people to ever use an interviewer. I think that was not part of normal free-response experiments. In free-response—in the Rhine Lab, I am guessing—they would say, "There's a picture in the envelope. Could be anything. Tell me about it." A person would have to do that. If they had never done it before, they would guess, as you did.

Mishlove: [laughs] Yeah.

The CIA then asked us to train up a group of Army people. The Army was getting embarrassed having to come to California whenever they needed to find a Russian airplane or a submarine or a kidnapped general or some other thing. They wanted to be able to do it by themselves. So, Hal and I went to a meeting prepared for us where there were thirty Army officers, all to take part in a remote viewing task. These were men who were willing to volunteer and contribute despite the possibility of jeopardizing their chance for promotion as remote viewers. We chose six of these men. The star of that group was Joe McMoneagle. He was, again, one of the most psychic people we'd ever seen. There were six people in the group who had never done remote viewing before. We did six trials with each of them. Each day for six days, Hal and the commanding officer, Colonel Scotty Watt, would go hide somewhere. The person of the day would just be faced with a piece of paper and me. [I would] say, "Okay, Scotty and Hal have gone to hide someplace." They could be in a bowling alley or a boat dock or a church or anything, anything in the Bay Area. We did six trials with each of these six guys, so we did thirty-six trials. Since their rank order matched, best to worst, you would expect each guy to get one right. So you would expect six first place matches, one from each of the six people. We got nineteen first place matches, to the odds of one in a million for this group of people. They were highly significant.

If you wanted to measure the effect size, you take the number of standard deviations. In this case, it was four standard deviations, divided by the square root of the number of trials. It is four sigma divided by the number of trials equals the square root of thirty-six. So, the effect size is four divided by six, or two thirds. That's a phenomenally high effect size. An effect size of 0.67—that is twenty times greater than card guessing or Ganzfeld. It was remarkable. People could hardly believe it. In fact, the program carried on for another decade with these people seeing effect size in the 0.4 to 0.5 range, which was a new super high ground in psychic ability. Two of these were very high scores: one came from a group of Army officers who had never done this before; the other was our control subject. So, the control subject and the six Army officers are the ones who staked out the new high ground for psychic abilities with people who were inexperienced, off the street, never done this before. They were showing psychic functioning at least ten times higher than is normally seen. So, the idea is that remote viewing in this free response format of a viewer working with the interviewer may be a new approach that can tease out reliable and useful aspects of this hitherto fairly random phenomenon.

Mishlove: I gather that the six Army trainees that you had—well, I'm calling them trainees, but I gather that you gave them a minimal amount of training. You basically just told them what to do, rather than how to do it. Of course, those are words, and we're dealing with an internal mental process. People must learn through trial and error how to avoid [those things].

Targ: That's right. If someone asks you, "What are you experiencing?" The answer is not "Macy's," the answer is a pictorial representation. This is not a new idea. The Buddhist teacher Padmasambhava, the master teacher of 800 AD, talks about self-liberation through seeing with naked awareness. It sounds like remote viewing. He said, as you expand your awareness into the timeless regions, you must give up your desire to name things. You must give up naming, give up grasping, and that was completely understood 1,200 years ago.

Mishlove: As I believe you pointed out to me that there are other Buddhist scriptures going back even further that describe this process in some detail. What's unique about the modern era is that the materialistic metaphysics is so strong that some people would just throw up their hands and say, "You know, Jeffrey and Russell must be absolutely crazy to talk about this."

Targ: One of the things that was supportive of our work is that shortly after we published our findings in all the journals, then the Soviet Union became interested. I went to Russia in 1983 and 1984 and found university laboratories doing remote viewing just like what we had done with the same kind of results that we saw.

Mishlove: As I recall, you conducted a long-distance experiment between Russia and the US.

Targ: That's right. We worked with a Russian healer named Eugenia Davitashvili [1949-2015], where she was able to describe where somebody was hiding in San Francisco. As we sat with her, my daughter, Elisabeth [1961-2002], the Russian translator, interviewed her in Russian to try and get Eugenia to tell us where our friend was hiding, and Eugenia did excellently 6,000 miles away.

Mishlove: It would seem as if we're talking about an ability, which is not constrained either by time or space.

Targ: That's right. Modern physics is very interested in the idea of—I was going to say, timeless awareness, [but] really, it's living in a non-local space-time. That is, there are physics experiments that indicate that photons that are born together and travel away from one another at the speed of light. If you grab one of the photons the other one notices it. It's as though the photons are coherent when they're born so that one twin notices that the other one was detected.

Mishlove: Yes, Einstein thought that such a thing would be impossible. He conjectured that quantum theory could not be true because it would imply what he called the "spooky action at a distance."

Targ: That's right. In 1960, John Stewart Bell published a paper saying that the non-local theory of physics could not be correct; [that] quantum mechanics forbids that. Then, in the 1970s, several people did experiments showing that, indeed, photons generated together are entangled, just as Schrödinger had said much earlier. They're entangled so that if you grab one photon, the other one notices. Much like identical twins. There's a whole literature of identical twins born together and reared apart, and they have shockingly similar lives in many cases.

Mishlove: All of this suggests that if we're going to have a scientific theory that can explain psychic functioning, we must start with an understanding that everything is interconnected; that the very idea of separation is something of an illusion created by our minds.

Targ: The Buddhists were happy to tell you, 2,500 years ago, that separation is an illusion, at least in consciousness. They're aware that hands and people can be separated, but for consciousness, there is no separation.

Mishlove: When the mystics say, "I'm one with everything," they're speaking ultimately a profound truth.

Targ: So it seems.

Mishlove: Not only a profound truth, but one that has not only scientific implications, but [also] practical implications as your work with the Army proved to have.

Targ: We went on to do this work with the Army, and they expanded that. The Army program went on for another fifteen years until 1995, where the whole program disappeared mysteriously. The Secretary of the Army, Robert Gates, said, "Since this program has never turned out any useful material, we're going to cancel the program." Shortly before that the CIA had published a release saying that of the 800 remote viewings done by the Army at Fort Meade, half of them were of intelligence applications. We really don't know what Bob Gates had in mind unless they had taken the whole program inside and are doing this in the basement of the CIA now.

We know that the CIA was somewhat afraid of the remote viewers, as though they had created a Frankenstein monster that had powers beyond their ability to control. You had Pat Price, who could read things at a distance, describe what was going on inside buildings, and focus the attention inside the code room of a foreign embassy. Price could do all sorts of astonishing things, which he did for the CIA after they hired him away from us, and he really frightened them.

Mishlove: All the good research you did at SRI, as you pointed out in a previous interview, was highly significant for a long period of time. You were working with people who didn't consider themselves psychic, but they were successful professionals.

Targ: That's right.

Mishlove: CIA monitors, military ...

Targ: Two CIA agents came to investigate what our protocols were, and I put them to work as I always did. I said, "If you want to see what we're doing, you be the subject. I will show you how to do it, and we'll send someone off to hide." Both did extremely well. In one case, the travelers went to a windmill locked with a big padlock. The man I was interviewing was an expert lock picker, and his whole interview was about the nature of the padlock, but he didn't see the windmill. He saw where the padlock was, how it was attached, and how he would break in.

Mishlove: It certainly suggests that people who think of themselves as psychic, or people who are not fully adult humans, like college students, are not going to do as well, in these kinds of tests, as individuals who have experienced a measure of success in their lives.

Targ: That's right. One of the things that comes out of our conversation is that in the work we did at SRI was light-hearted. We expected success during every trial, and we were rewarded with an uncommon degree of success.

Mishlove: Russell, once again, our time is up. Fortunately, I know you're going to be with me for a couple more days. We have much more to talk about. Thank you once again.

Targ: Very happy to be with you.

4

Precognition

Recorded on March 2, 2017

Jeffrey Mishlove: Today, we're going to explore precognition, cognizing the future. With me is my dear old friend, Russell Targ, a laser physicist, and author of many books. Russell is the co-founder of the remote viewing program at SRI International, a major US military industrial think tank. Welcome, Russell.

Russell Targ: Happy to be here with you.

Mishlove: It's a pleasure once again to be with you and to talk about one of the most fascinating topics in the field of parapsychology: precognition. I know you have had some precognitive dreams that were very meaningful to you.

Targ: Yes, I have. I think precognition is the most interesting of the psychic abilities and it may turn out to be that precognition is the senior ability that drives all the others.

Mishlove: I know our friend Ed May believes that's the case and I have a couple of interviews with him in the catalog about that topic.

Targ: Yes, I understood that.

I once got into a security problem, which will amuse you. I was working with one of the remote viewers from the Army who wasn't getting anywhere. This was our first meeting. He said, "You know, I close my eyes and it's dark. I just don't see anything." We did that for about 20 minutes. I told him, "In 10 minutes, they're going to be coming back here, and then we'll take you to the place. Why don't you just quiet your mind and visualize what it's going to look like when they come back, and we go to this place? Because you're going to then experience it. What do you experience now regarding where we're going to be when they come back?" He said, "Oh, I can smell the water. There are birds flying around. I can see piers on the dock." And that was entirely correct. The woman who was typing this up was a security person for our group at SRI. She turned me in for precognition when I was supposed to be doing remote viewing. She wrote, "Targ was not following instructions."

Mishlove: But they got an accurate hit nonetheless because you allowed yourself to be guided by intuition.

Targ: I've had some dreams that seem quite illustrative of psychic abilities. They seem quite precognitive. I know that telling you about a dream is like telling you about my old acid trip. It's not so interesting. But some dreams about precognition just call for themselves to be related and explained.

Mishlove: Precognitions often occur in dreams. I think it's very significant.

Targ: To be worth relating, a precognitive dream must be free of wish fulfillment and anxiety. For example, if I dream about failing an exam that I haven't studied for, that would not be a precognitive dream because it's just what you would expect. On the other hand, if I were to dream this quite unusual, anxiety-free, and bizarre dream unlike any other experiences in my life and I relate it to someone, then it might be a candidate.

Mishlove: I think the fascinating thing about your dreams is that in advance of any confirmation, you sensed that this was precognitive for the very reasons you've just described.

Targ: Yes, I frequently have dreams at night and remember them. I think the task of a researcher is to definitively tell the difference between their precognitive dreams and their ordinary anxiety wish fulfillment dreams. For me to get credit in the big book of precognitive dreams, I have to relate that dream to my wife, Patricia, before I tell it to anybody.

If I can't identify it as precognitive and don't wait for it to happen, well, I could miss it a million times in a lifetime.

Russell and Patricia at home, 2023.

A recent dream I had fulfills all those requirements very nicely. In my dream, I had gone to the bank with my wife to the safe deposit vault where I had been once when we opened an account. I saw a bright silver faceplate used to put over an unused light switch. I took out my Swiss Army knife and unscrewed the single screw holding this to the wall and I put the screw and the faceplate in my pocket and left. I was worried about being arrested for stealing something from the bank, of course.

Mishlove: There was an emotional component.

Targ: That's right. In the dream I went to the Golden Gate Bridge, which is 30 miles north of where I lived, and I thought about throwing the faceplate into the ocean. I realized that this place was full of cameras, so I might be photographed disposing of the stolen faceplate. I decided to go to McDonald's to wrap it up with a napkin and dispose of it there. I got to McDonald's and I realized that I couldn't do that either because my fingerprints were all over it. I decided to go home to scour the fingerprints off. I washed the faceplate with soap and water, but I was worried that the oil from the fingerprints wouldn't come off. I used some acetone to scrub the faceplate and then went under the sink to get a kitchen cleanser. As I was looking for the cleanser, I woke up all in a twitter from having this crazy dream.

Mishlove: It's an unusual dream that you would focus so much on cleaning this object.

Targ: Cleaning fingerprints. Never had such a bizarre dream. I couldn't relate it to anything in my life. I told Patricia about it and she also thought it was a very unusual dream. About five hours later I got a Federal Express package. I opened it up and inside was a thin glass plate that I had ordered to be the faceplate for my cell phone.

Mishlove: Which also is a camera.

Targ: It's also a camera. I had forgotten that I had ordered it a week or ten days before it arrived. When I pulled it out, there were warnings to stop and read the instructions. They were all about how to remove fingerprints from the faceplate and the cell phone screen. The package had three different liquids and an abrasive used to make sure every fingerprint is removed because otherwise the new faceplate wouldn't seat properly. There was also a six-minute video on exactly how to make sure you've scrubbed off every fingerprint. I realized that the faceplate is so fragile, and they made sure to say that there is only one chance to seat it correctly. Because my vision is poor, it was not a good job to lay down this thin fragile thing.

I asked Patricia, who's a clear-sighted woman, "Could you please watch this video and then help me scrub everything clean?" Which she did. She got packet one and cleaned it and packet two and cleaned it and then carefully laid down the faceplate.

Mishlove: So many elements of the dream occurred unexpectedly and within hours of receiving the faceplate for your phone.

Targ: Yes, and in detail. I've never had a dream about fingerprints. I dare say very few people, unless they're a safe cracker, can imagine having a dream all about fingerprints. I thought that this was an unusually clear example of a precognitive dream occurring the evening before being stimulated by events the following day. It didn't cross my mind that this was a precognitive dream until later in the day when I read a biography of Wolf Messing, the great Russian psychic. He had startlingly accurate precognitive dreams the day of—or week before—an event. He and Stalin became friends and Stalin would rely on Wolf Messing to give him information even though Messing was Jewish and Stalin was very allergic to Jews.

Mishlove: But when you told your wife about it early in the morning at that point you thought it might be precognitive.

Targ: When I woke up, I immediately told Patricia I had a dream that really made no sense at all but was very accurate. You could have a dream that's very accurate but also anxiety producing such as the wheel coming off the car or something. However, this was unrelated to anything like that.

Mishlove: It's odd in a way, though, because it's not as if cleaning off the faceplate is a very significant event in your life.

Targ: It was anxiety producing because I couldn't see well enough to do it. In fact, the faceplate of a wall switch is almost the same size as the faceplate of the cellphone. My subconscious must have dredged up stealing a faceplate from the bank as my looking for something the size of this piece of glass.

Mishlove: I'm reminded of a book you're probably familiar with by J.W. Dunne called *An Experiment with Time*.

Targ: I published that book with Hampton Roads as part of my *Studies in Consciousness* series.

Mishlove: I didn't mention earlier that you've published a series of classic books, and this is one of them. He was an Oxford don, as I recall, who analyzed many peoples' dreams, comparing the imagery in them to events in the future and in the past. He found that the future seemed to influence those dreams as much as past events.

Mishlove: Backwards causality is one way to look at it.

Targ: A very hot topic in modern physics. There have been three conferences on retrocausality at the University of California in San Diego. They were not particularly stimulated by extrasensory perception research but, in modern physics, there's more and more evidence that, in certain cases, things occurring in the future can affect the past.

Mishlove: I know one of the important principles in theoretical physics is symmetry; the idea being that if time, events, or particles move forward in time there ought to be processes, waves, or particles that move [in] the other direction.

Targ: That makes us nervous because it seems to interfere with free will. If you have a dream about something occurring, does it have to happen? My feeling about that is that there is free will but much less than you might imagine. Basically, as a physicist, I believe in determinism. If the wheel falls off your car it's because the nuts came loose and not because of some psychic occurrence. If you dream about the wheel coming off the car, that might have been stimulated by subconsciously noticing that the nuts were loose. I think that you can use precognitive dream to avoid having the catastrophic experience signified by the dream.

An example of that was on 9/11 when the four airplanes crashed because of the terrorists hijacking them. All those planes had half or fewer of the normal capacity of passengers.

Mishlove: That's one example of several others we could cite. Parapsychologists have looked at train crashes and have found that—

Targ: William Cox [1915-1994] had a similar observation involving train crashes on the East Coast. He discovered that after normalizing for bad weather or holidays, trains that crashed had fewer people on them than trains that didn't. You apparently can't prevent the train from crashing, but you don't have to participate in the experience.

Mishlove: It certainly suggests that at a subliminal level, the human mind is scanning for possible dangers in the environment including in the future. No doubt the people who avoided being on those planes and trains were not necessarily conscious about why they made those decisions.

Targ: Subsequently, a number of those who opted not to be passengers were interviewed. They claimed they had a bad feeling and didn't know why.

Mishlove: We call it a premonition.

Targ: That's right, or presentiment, which is a premonition of usually something bad.

Mishlove: Which brings up another whole line of research in parapsychology. Stimuli are presented to experimental subjects and physiological measurements are made showing that the body can react in advance of the presentation of the stimuli even though they're presented in a random order.

Targ: If you're going to hear a loud noise in the future your physiology shows in advance that you're going to experience this loud unpleasant noise. Your body knows that something is going to happen to you.

Mishlove: It's very possible that this process, backward causality, is happening all the time around us. It's not just the occasional precognitive dream, which is very visible to us, but at a subliminal level we're always receiving influences from the future.

Targ: We examined that in a controlled way at SRI. In our experiments we had subjects in the laboratory describing where some other people were going to hide. In one instance, I was sitting in the shielded room with Pat Price [1918-1975], who was one of our prodigiously successful remote viewers and was a psychic policeman. Hal and the contract monitor had gone to hide. Price said, "I'd like a cup of coffee. We don't have to wait for them to get there. Why don't I just tell you right now where they're going to be in a half hour, and we can leave and get some coffee." I thought that was a novel idea. He had shown himself to be remarkably psychic in earlier instances. So, I say, "Okay, Pat, what do you see?" He said, "I see them going out on a pier. I see little boats with their masts stepped and there are other boats ready to go sailing. Off to the right there's something that looks like a Chinese restaurant with a lawn in front of it. So, they've gone to some sort of boat dock near a restaurant. Let's get out of here." Forty-five minutes later, Hal and the monitor returned from the Redwood City Marina, which is exactly as Price described it. There is a little boat jetty that had boats with their masts up and others with the masts stepped and a regular American restaurant with a hanging hill roof like a Chinese restaurant might have with grass in front of it.

Redwood City marina.

When I was in the Soviet Union in 1983, the people at Yerevan, Soviet Armenia, had replicated our experiments. A psychiatrist named Ruben Poghosyan had done a whole series of experiments. From time to time, the remote viewer would start talking before the traveler is at the site. I said we'd experienced that as well.

Mishlove: And of course, in a true precognition experiment, the description is made before even any kind of flip of the coin or random process occurs to determine what the target will be.

Targ: Yes. We had submitted a paper to the IEEE, the Engineering Society. After long negotiations, teaching the IEEE editors and engineering colleagues how to remote view and so forth, they'd agreed to publish our paper. It required jumping through many hoops. As we were typing up the final form of this paper, I proposed to Hal, "You know, we're not writing about precognition because we think that's too far out for the IEEE. I think we should include it because we saw it." And he said, "We haven't done a formal study," though we were very confident that we had witnessed it. We were living in a psychic bubble in the late 1970s. Every experiment we did was successful, significant, and publishable. There were no missed experiments.

Mishlove: You've had this amazing track record that almost nobody in the field of parapsychology has been able to equal, which is one of the reasons I'm very pleased to have you here.

Targ: That's the way our remarkable decade went. We published all our findings, and tried to tell people everything we knew about it. The researcher, Professor Robert John at Princeton, was able to replicate this quite well over a 20-year period. He did lots of precognitive experiments.

Mishlove: The literature in parapsychology includes—it must be a hundred precognitive experiments.

Targ: We did not invent the idea of precognition, but we had a lot of it in our experiments, often under very good control. In 1982, as our work became more and more classified, I left SRI because it was no longer possible to publish anything though it was in our agreement that we could publish stuff that wasn't classified. They just assumed this whole program was top secret.

Mishlove: I know you entered another great adventure in your life at that period, but we're running out of time right now, Russell. We'll have to come back and talk about your silver futures forecasting work, as well as some of the theoretical work you've done in complex space, and how that relates to precognition.

Mishlove: Precognition is always into the future, isn't it?

Targ: I think that that's true. There are a lot of variables we don't understand.

Mishlove: You have tried to develop some theoretical models that could account for precognition.

Targ: A model that I put together with Elizabeth Rauscher, who is a physicist from UC Berkeley.

Mishlove: Who also has been a guest on *New Thinking Allowed*.

Targ: We have a model based on Hermann Minkowski's [1864-1909] ideas from the early 20th century. Einstein's theory of relativity is a wonderful correct model of the way the universe works. Other people, such as Fitzgerald and Lorentz were aware that there was something the matter with the geometrical model of the world at the end of the 19th century. Einstein couldn't solve the equations until Minkowski came along and said, why don't we do this in a complex four-dimensional metric? You have three space dimensions, x, y, and z, up, down, and sideways, and a complex time dimension.

Mishlove: When you say complex, we're really talking about the square root of minus one, which is an imaginary number. But when you add that into an equation, it opens whole new realms.

Targ: It gives you another dimension in which to work. The four-dimensional Minkowski space with complex, imaginary time, allowed Einstein to solve his equations for special relativity. What Elizabeth, our friend Gary Feinberg [1933-1992]—chairman of the physics department at Columbia—and I one day spelled out on his blackboard was the equation of a complete complex space-time. All our dimensions, up, down, sideways, and time, are all complex quantities so we're not adding in another dimension nor are we saying ESP is in the fourth dimension. We're saying that we have a familiar three-space and one-time dimension that works quite well forecasting the tides and the eclipses, and it might be that all those dimensions are complex quantities. We make use of an imaginary component when designing alternating current circuits, so it's nothing unusual for a scientist.

Minkowski's original space-time for Einstein was eight-dimensional complex space having some of the things that we see now in modern physics, like non-local space-time. In non-local space-time, there are cases where you can generate a pair of photons in the same experiment, and, when the photons go off in opposite directions, they're entangled. As Schrödinger predicted, if you grab one photon, the other photon is correlated with it so that no matter what you do to the one photon, you see an appropriate change in the other photon.

Mishlove: One photon sneezes, and the other one catches a cold.

Targ: It's like identical twins that are raised apart. They often have shockingly similar lives. What we're predicting is that in one example of a manifold that gives you this kind of non-local connection is called the "Complex Minkowski Space." That eight-space model's property is that there is always a path from, say, me sitting here today to Jeffrey sitting somewhere else tomorrow. They go along a path through the distance and the time separating us, so that if you add up this x squared plus that y squared, they'll add to zero. That's because some of the x's and some of the y's are negative, and some are complex. In the eight-space model, there is an infinite number of paths that connect today and here and now with tomorrow and some other place.

Mishlove: In other words, this model is a mathematical demonstration of what mystics have been saying all along: that everything is connected.

Targ: People could avoid car accidents, and getting on airplanes that are going to crash. I've had experiences like that on my motorcycle, while riding to work, as I did every day. As I was riding down this quite nice parkway, swinging down this curve it occurred to me, what if there was a board across the road? There'd be no way for me to stop. I started to slow down, going over toward the curb. By the time I got around the corner, there was indeed a two-by-four sitting in the road, but I was going slowly enough so I could drive over it. That was really a rewarding experience for my being aware of the precognition. A parapsychologist might say that it was just clairvoyance because I looked into the future and saw it was around the corner. But, as I read it at the time, I was going to hit a board, and I wanted to make that as mild an experience as I could.

Mishlove: Thank you for being with me, Russell.

Targ: Thank you.

5

Precognitive Financial Forecasting

Recorded on March 3, 2017

Jeffrey Mishlove: Today we are going to look at the use of precognitive remote viewing in financial forecasting. With me is my old and dear friend, Russell Targ, who is a laser physicist and a parapsychologist. Russell is the co-founder of the remote viewing program that ran for many years at SRI International in Menlo Park, California, a major military-industrial think tank. Welcome, Russell.

Russell Targ: Thank you very much. I'm happy to be with you.

Mishlove: It's a pleasure to be with you. You achieved great fame. I think it was back in the 1980s, when you used precognition for forecasting silver futures. It was on the front page of the *Wall Street Journal*; you were so successful.

MONDAY, OCTOBER 22. 1984

THE WALL STREET JOURNAL.

© 1984 Dow Jones & Company, Inc. All Rights Reserved.

> Did Psychic Powers
> Give Firm a Killing
> In the Silver Market?

Front page, *Wall Street Journal*, October 22, 1984.

Targ: When I left SRI, the program had just become totally top secret, so I could not publish anything anymore, and that was not for me. I didn't go to graduate school to become a psychic spy for the CIA, so I left SRI and formed an organization called Delphi Associates, which were making toys for Atari, and forecasting silver markets.

Mishlove: Named after the famous oracle in Greece.

Targ: We were working with an experienced psychic, a broker, and an investor to keep separate the parts of the forecasting to prevent contamination by any one person knowing too much. The idea was to forecast changes in the silver commodity markets a week in advance using something called associative remote viewing. You can't read the numbers on the big board at the commodity exchange in New York and say, ah, silver is going from $8 to $9, so buy silver.

Mishlove: In other words, numbers don't come through as well as colors, shapes, textures, or forms in remote viewing.

Targ: It's very hard to remote view anything analytical because ESP is a non-analytical ability, so we call our trick *associative* remote viewing. The broker, each week, would choose four objects in his office and associate each one with a market change: up a lot, up a little, down a lot, down a little. Because of the trading range of a commodity called December silver, he said the trading range should be $0.25. So, he would have four objects: say a book, a perfume bottle, a coffee cup, and his leftover pancake from breakfast. Those are the four objects, different objects.

Mishlove: They must be very distinct from each other.

Targ: One represents up a little, one up a lot, one down a little, or one down a lot. I never knew what the objects were, and they would vary from week to week. I would sit with my viewer, such as you, and say, "All right, Jeffrey, here we are on Monday. On Friday, I will hand you an object. I have no idea what it's going to be." We're not talking about the market. We're just talking about what object I'm going to give you next Friday.

Mishlove: An object you are going to hand me in the future.

Targ: That's right. I'd say, "Quiet your mind, and imagine that it's Friday now, and I'm putting something in your hand. What do you experience?" And you might say to me, "I see something round, and it's kind of floppy, and it's got a weird smell. That's what I get. I have a strange object, kind of disgusting." I would say, "That's a terrific description. There's nothing analytical there. It's all direct experience. Thank you. I will call the broker and see if he's got anything like that." I call the broker and say, "I've got a pretty good description. What are your objects?" He says, "I've got this perfume bottle, a book, a coffee cup, and my leftover pancake." I say, "I think we've got a wonderful description of your pancake. It's this round, floppy object with a kind of odd smell." He says, "I think so too." I say, "What does that mean?" He says, "That's the down-a-lot object. Based on your viewer describing my leftover pancake, we'll sell $50,000 worth of silver into the rising market. It's rising because the Hunch brothers are buying silver, but because you saw a pancake, we're going to sell silver instead." That was one of our biggest successes. The market fell like a rock for some unknown reason that week, but we made tens of thousands of dollars on that one trade.

Mishlove: As I recall, you had nearly a 100% track record.

Targ: We made nine calls, one a week for nine weeks, and each of them was correct. We made $120,000 in nine weeks. No errors.

Mishlove: That ought to be enough to convince anybody to keep doing it.

Targ: The following year, we were not successful because a variety of inadvertencies occurred. The investor who had put up the money quite generously, and which he shared with us, said, "I think we've cornered the market. We're going to make a ton of money. Let's do it twice a week." Bad idea, because doing it twice a week meant that the viewer did not get feedback for trial one until after trial two. The experiment is still open from the viewer's point of view, and he must do another experiment without getting feedback.

Mishlove: The feedback from the first trial might, in some way, contaminate the next one.

Targ: We had several misses. In addition, we weren't using nice little objects anymore. We thought it would be easier to use pictures of places rather than objects. That's something we often experience. A researcher says, "We tried to replicate your experiment, and it didn't work." And I say, "What did you change?" There are always three or four things that they have changed, so it isn't a replication.

Mishlove: To me, the crucial thing in your research, since you've been so very successful, is *Russell Targ*. Nobody else can replicate that.

Targ: The fact that we failed in year two doesn't take away the 100,000 to one odds in year one.

Mishlove: Nor the money you made.

Targ: Nor the money we made.

Mishlove: Also, our mutual friend, Marty Rosenblatt, has been pursuing this line of research now for over a decade, hundreds of trials over more than ten years, and he has consistently reported a hit rate about 60%, when you'd only expect 50% by chance.

Targ: I can tell you an interesting story about Marty's experiment. Several of his viewers all started describing the wrong target ever since the 2016 election. I'll reveal my political feelings—it's as though the whole psychic atmosphere is contaminated because of the election. All the things that used to work during the previous sunny nine months all changed and his experiment is not working presently.

Mishlove: I think it's fair to say that proponents and opponents and foreign observers around the world were all pretty much in shock because of what has happened. The psychic atmosphere globally has changed.

Targ: Certainly, that psychic barometer has changed, and I thought that was quite amazing to hear.

Mishlove: Well, that may eventually recover.

Targ: Oh, I'm sure it'll recover. It does not wipe out his winnings, nor does it wipe out the successful statistical significance of his past years of work. But it was a great coincidence that something happened to the psychic atmosphere.

Mishlove: It also points out that there are human emotional variables that affect this kind of functioning. Precognition is a mystery in and of itself, but one thing we know is that when the human mind is agitated, psychic functioning is typically diminished.

Targ: The Buddha said again and again in the Prajnaparamita written around 500 BC, that separation is an illusion, at least for consciousness. The reason you can describe something, for instance a change in the market, is not that a message is sent to you, but rather you have direct apprehension of what's going to happen on the floor of the commodity exchange next Friday.

Mishlove: In effect, you are it.

Targ: That's right.

Mishlove: You are it, which seems to go totally against our normal ego understanding of who we are as biological creatures. At the level of consciousness, we may be something vastly different.

Targ: I mentioned that Daryl Bem had done some exciting experiments that were very, very successful.

Mishlove: Could we summarize what he's done for the benefit of our readers who may not be familiar with his work?

Targ: Daryl Bem did a series of very simple experiments. For example, there would be on the computer screen, a picture of two brick walls. One of the brick walls will crumble away, showing an image behind it. The idea is to touch the screen corresponding to the brick wall that will crumble away beforehand.

Mishlove: The computer chooses it at random.

Targ: After you touch the screen, the computer randomly decides which wall to dissolve. You're not asked to touch the one that is programmed to dissolve; you're going to have to touch the one, which, in the future, the computer will obliterate for you. The college men who were used as subjects were very successful touching the screen that was going to dissolve.

Mishlove: I know he had several other psychological tasks.

Targ: The interesting thing is that men were most successful at correctly identifying the screens that were concealing pornographic pictures. So, if there's a pornographic picture in your future, and you're a college sophomore, you will be more successful at correctly touching that screen than if it's an ocean sunset. This didn't work for women at all.

Mishlove: So, there's a psychological motivation.

Targ: In experiments, you always like to find a difference. In this case, the men were extremely successful [at] finding those targets even though they had to look into the future to get their picture. This has now been replicated in ninety laboratories across the world, at odds of billions to one. It's very easy to do, just pop this program in the computer, and the subjects will happily tap the screen that will have the desired picture to be chosen by the computer in the future.

Mishlove: It's like the experiments with the mice that stimulate their own pleasure centers.

Targ: That's right.

Mishlove: It suggests when experiments are highly replicable, which this one seems to be from your description, although I've heard other accounts ...

Targ: He calls his experiment "Feeling the Future."

Mishlove: There ought to be some practical applications that emerge from it, as with your silver futures forecasting.

Mishlove: Our late colleague, Douglas Dean who had been at the Newark School of Engineering, did a fascinating study at a conference with business executives. It's all written up in his book, *Executive ESP,* where he compared the precognitive abilities on a simple computerized test of business executives and CEOs. He contrasted those whose companies were profitable with those whose companies were losing money. He found a very clear difference, that the profitable CEOs scored high on precognition, and those executives whose companies were losing money showed what we call "psi missing." They had a statistically significant score in the opposite direction.

Targ: I have always had the feeling that if I were to look for someone kidnapped in San Francisco, I would not look for the most psychic girl selling flowers on the street. Instead, I would go to the president of the Bank of America because he's somebody who is accustomed to making decisions in the absence of perfect data, and he's shown he can do it; whereas the young woman would probably be very attached to getting the correct answer and would worry about being embarrassed.

Mishlove: Would it be the case that every parapsychologist could achieve that level of certitude, it would probably make a big difference in the field.

Targ: Charlie Tart, Marilyn Schlitz and William Braud are a handful of experimenters who had success all through their careers.

Mishlove: That's important, and it's wonderful, and I wish we could understand more some of the inner psychological dynamics. I know, in my own case, it's been more mixed. But in any case, Russell, it's been a great pleasure being with you once again. Thank you so much.

Targ: Thank you very much for the opportunity. I'm happy to be here.

6

Non-Duality

~

Recorded on March 3, 2017

Jeffrey Mishlove: We'll be exploring the philosophy of non-duality, or Advaita. You might think of that as an Indian Hindu philosophy, but it has implications in both Eastern and Western thought. With me is Russell Targ, [who is] a laser physicist, a pioneer parapsychologist, and co-founder of the remote viewing research program at SRI International. Welcome, Russell.

Russell Targ: Very happy to be with you.

Mishlove: I'm happy to be with you as well. I forgot to say by way of introduction that you are an old and very good friend. We've spent many, many hours together discussing subjects like non-duality, so it's a pleasure to be able to share that conversation with our larger audience.

Targ: Like getting older every year.

Mishlove: What really impresses me the most about your interest in non-duality is, first, it can provide an underpinning for people working in remote viewing and in parapsychology. Second, you're very good about tracing the origins of non-dualistic thinking in both Eastern and Western thought.

Targ: Now, Schrödinger said we are all connected. Because of his Advaita feelings, he felt that separation is an illusion.

Mishlove: There is only one consciousness, not multiple.

Targ: That's right.

Mishlove: Which sort of goes against our commonsense experience. Most of us live our lives believing we are separate from each other.

Targ: That's right. Schrödinger felt there was no separation. He thought that consciousness was fundamental. You might say he was an idealist. In Buddhism, there's a problem with idealism. The idealists, in Buddhism, tend to believe that everything is mind. And on the other track are the materialists, saying it's all material. The middle ground people, in line with Nāgārjuna, who wrote during the time of Christ, felt most things are neither this nor, not this. So, in a lot of the writings of Buddhism, in the Heart Sutra and the Diamond Sutra, you run into statements that are inexplicable. That is, from a dualistic framework. There's no way to understand it, and most people just read over them. A student asks of Buddha, in the Diamond Sutra, "Will this teaching be known in a hundred years from now?" And Buddha's response is, this is neither a teaching nor not a teaching. Take that, you so and so. [Laughter]

Nāgārjuna, who was really named—I always mispronounce this, Nāgārjuna. The Nagas were the sea creatures that were his friends, and his other name was really Arjuna. So, he's known as Nāgārjuna. He is the one who said that most things are neither true nor not true. And all our suffering is due to Aristotle. I don't know if Nāgārjuna said that, but I attribute it to him.

Mishlove: You're paraphrasing. But there is a possibility, as we discussed earlier, that Nāgārjuna was exposed to some of the philosophy of Aristotle. Alexander the Great, a student of Aristotle, brought his armies all the way into India, I think, several years before Nāgārjuna.

Targ: As I read Nāgārjuna, I came to the idea that his teaching was really. Aristotle creates a lot of suffering because, in the entire Western pantheon, we believe a thing is either true or it is not true.

Mishlove: Or if it's neither true nor not true, then it's meaningless.

Targ: That's right. Aristotle is possibly most famous for his law of the excluded middle. It's either white or it's not white. There's no gray in Aristotle's teachings. That lack of the middle, I mean, this is the law of the excluded middle. It's the basis of all science. I've either proved it, or I haven't proved it. It's either turned on or it's not turned on.

Mishlove: But in recent years, we've seen the development of new forms of logic. For example, I understand that in fields like optics, with precision telescopes and so on, they operate on what is known as fuzzy logic. There is the possibility of neither true nor false.

Targ: That's right. There's a big area of computational theory. Nāgārjuna said that suffering comes from the exclusion of the middle. He said in our lives, almost everything we experience is in the gray area, neither true nor not true. For example, in the mind-body situation, he would consider—I consider that a false dichotomy. As a physicist, I'm resistant to being engaged in mind-body conversations anyway. I discovered Nāgārjuna fifty years ago when I was a graduate student at Columbia. I once ran into a teacher there who was passionate about Nāgārjuna. She felt he was an unsung hero of world thought.

Mishlove: You've also pointed out to me, earlier, that the writings of Nāgārjuna are rather like the physical science concept of complementarity, like the wave-particle duality.

Targ: My understanding of non-duality is that it was brought to the fore by Nāgārjuna, who was considered the second Buddha and wrote many books starting 100 years after Jesus. I wrote a book about the teachings of Nāgārjuna called *The End of Suffering, or How to Get Out of Hell Free*. Nāgārjuna considered that suffering occurs but it's not necessary. What I think he pointed out is that all of our suffering is really due to Aristotle. Now, Nāgārjuna would not say that, but I think that that's where he's coming from. Aristotle taught, most famously, the excluded middle by saying the thing can be true, or it can be false, it can be black, or it can be white, a man or a woman, and that's it. Today we know the excluded middle philosophy is the source of a lot of suffering. Nāgārjuna was aware—he was a brilliant logician and grammarian—that there was a lot of confusion over the dualistic way of seeing the world.

Mishlove: Something can't be both A and not A at the same time.

Targ: What Nāgārjuna taught is a four-point view that a thing can be true, it can be false, a small number of things can be true and false, and most things are neither true nor false. For example, in modern physics, 2,000 years after Nāgārjuna, Niels Bohr observed that light has a dual nature. Light can be a photon that, when it goes into my camera, it triggers the light meter, which counts one photon at a time, and it has no wave quality at all. When light goes through the lens, it makes a beautiful color image. If it goes through a prism, it makes a spectrum as Newton showed. A second prism next to the first prism will reassemble the light rays from a rainbow back to white; perfectly wave-like behavior.

A high school student studying light knows all about the waves. A college student will notice that light has a wave property some of the time when they're doing a prism experiment and has a particle quality when they're counting photons with a photomultiplier. Einstein observed the quantum nature of light—for which he got a Nobel Prize—by showing that the energy of light is the frequency of light times Planck's constant for all frequencies, and the energy has nothing to do with how much light there is. The energy of light pertains to its frequency, and that was a great observation.

Mishlove: When we look at light, the frequency really is the color of the light.

Targ: Each frequency has a color. Niels Bohr, around 1910, the time of Einstein, enunciated the principle of complementarity: light has a dual nature, the wave nature or particle nature, and what you see depends on the instrument. You can't say that light is a wave or a particle. It sounds like a real question, but it's not. What Nāgārjuna had pointed out is that there are lots of questions like that. The "Are you a boy or a girl?" question causes a lot of suffering today, for example, as we know that there's a continuum from male to female with very fine gradations.

The mind-body problem is also a non-question. Is mind made of the same stuff as bodies? People have argued about that since the time of Descartes. The Cartesian view of mind-body separation has also caused a lot of suffering, but mainly for philosophers.

Mishlove: You mentioned Niels Bohr, and my understanding is that he selected a family coat of arms that contains this symbol, the yin-yang.

Targ: How very interesting.

Mishlove: I think he saw that as a way of expressing his own thinking about what he called, as you say, complementarity.

Targ: That's very nice to know. The yin-yang was developed in China about 300 years before Nāgārjuna, showing that separations are apparent but not real. That is, in every red there's some green; in every green there's some red. The division often causes suffering.

Mishlove: Everything contains within it the seed of its own opposite.

Targ: Ramana Maharshi, who is a contemporary teacher, taught Advaita Vedanta; Advaita being an interesting choice of words. Ramana Maharshi's principal teaching is that we should quiet our minds and discover who we are, and the discovery of a quiet mind is that you are one with nature or one with God. The idea of Advaita in Sanskrit comes from division, and so teaching of "one with nature" or "one with the universe" there is no division. The word division comes from the devil, which is the idea that the devil is due to our suffering. Alan Watts, a great Buddhist teacher, used to say, whenever you make a separation, you make a mistake.

Mishlove: And create suffering to boot. It seems as if most people living their everyday lives are trapped in duality. We think in terms of good and evil, you want to hate the devil and love Jesus, for example: a world of love and hate, a world of right and wrong. It seems as if these things are fundamental to our moral existence.

Targ: That's certainly what Nāgārjuna taught; that is, he was trying to clear our minds. Buddhism as I understand it, is not a religion, but is a kind of teaching to diminish suffering. The purpose of life is to learn who we are and encounter our primordial spacious (sic) awareness, and then teach that. That would be a Dzogchen take on what we think we're doing.

Mishlove: I didn't mention for our readers that you are a practicing Buddhist, but we should also define the term you just used, Dzogchen.

Targ: I am indeed a practicing Buddhist, but I have no credential for teaching Buddhism. This has never stopped me, but you shouldn't take my word for it. If I'm telling you something different than you've been taught about Buddhism, you should consider both points of view.

Mishlove: The Buddha himself said something like that, as I recall. He said, test these ideas and see if they work for you.

Targ: The Buddha was aware of the dualistic problems in teaching. In his earliest consolidated writing, like in *The Diamond Sutra*, his student says, "Will this teaching be known hundreds of years from now?" Buddha said, "This is neither a teaching, nor not a teaching." I remember feeling great concern over that, having no idea what that could mean. It was Nāgārjuna who made me fall into alignment with the Buddhist teaching, because Nāgārjuna explained that most things are neither true nor not true. It's the so-called "two truths" teaching.

Mishlove: Back in the days of the Cold War, the great sociologist Pitirim Sorokin, who had founded the Department of Social Relations at Harvard University, but prior to that had been active in the Russian Revolution as a cabinet member of the Kerensky government, wrote about social conditions. He said of the US and the Soviet Union, the two great enemies of the Cold War, that we are not as good as we think we are, and they are not as bad as we think they are.

Targ: That's right. If only one idea comes out of this conversation, it is that the famous yin-yang symbol that you use and that we both share, is not a symbol of separation, nor is it showing the difference between the yin and the yang, but it is showing the non-dual nature, the non-separation of yin and yang.

Mishlove: I thank you for that, Russell, and I'm glad you bring it up, because not only do I wear this during our interviews, but the symbol appears in the introduction and the closing of each interview as well. I sometimes think, regarding this image, which is my own unique design, I added the rainbow colors to the yin-yang.

Targ: It's very handsome.

Mishlove: I think of it, if I had to take everything I've ever learned in my seven decades of life and put them into one image, this would be it.

Targ: It has worldwide agreement. It's agreement in modern philosophy, as many of the philosophers we revere, like Kurt Gödel, one of the great mathematicians of the 20th century, who brought us the incompleteness theorem. He said that you can have a great body of knowledge, and in that body of knowledge there will be true and things that are false. Also, in that body of knowledge there will always be some things whose truth simply cannot be ascertained; it's neither true nor not true, and there's no way within that group of sentences to understand it.

Mishlove: That no system of thought is ever capable of explaining itself.

Targ: Kurt Gödel sort of prepared us. Gödel was, again, one of the logical positivists. Many people think he and Wittgenstein were the greatest philosophers of the 20th century.

Mishlove: Well, he's very famous for his incompleteness theorem.

Targ: That's right. The incompleteness theorem says that any time you have a collection of postulates or ideas that are sufficiently complicated, there will be true sentences you can say, or, let's say, there are sentences you can say about your field. You cannot determine whether they are true or not true. I believe this is the current state of modern physics. I don't think people say this, but modern physics has enough indeterminate ideas or postulates, even starting with the two-slit interference.

Mishlove: Now, my reading of Gödel's incompleteness theorem has a bit of a different emphasis. I thought he was essentially saying that you cannot have any logical system of thought capable of explaining itself, including mind. If you want to explain anything, you must explain it from the outside, otherwise the explanation will be incomplete.

Targ: You can't know all about yourself if you have no place to stand. The incompleteness theorem says that any time you have a collection of postulates or ideas that are sufficiently complicated, there will be true sentences you can say, or let's say, there are sentences you can say about your field. You cannot determine whether they are true or not true. I believe this is the current state of modern physics. I don't think people say this, but modern physics has enough indeterminate ideas or postulates, even starting with the two-slit interference.

Mishlove: Now, my reading of Gödel's incompleteness theorem has a bit of a different emphasis. I thought he was essentially saying that you cannot have any logical system of thought capable of explaining itself, including mind. If you want to explain anything, you must explain it from the outside, otherwise the explanation will be incomplete.

Targ: You can't know all about yourself if you have no place to stand.

Targ: Ludwig Wittgenstein, who was a great teacher of mine and whom I have a great reverence for—unfortunately all my teachers are deceased—said that the riddle of the nature of man in time and space will be found outside of time and space.

Mishlove: Totally consistent with Gödel.

Targ: That's right.

Mishlove: You mentioned this term Dzogchen earlier, and we owe it to our readers to at least define the term.

Targ: There are three prominent paths in Buddhism. The Hinayana path, that teaches the Eightfold Way, which is a way of living life to diminish suffering, that is: right speech, where there's no lying and no gossip, right livelihood, so no guns, no alcohol, being aware of suffering in the world and being compassionate, and so forth.

The Mahayana path, the middle ground, teaches principally open-hearted bodhicitta experience. Bodhicitta means the Buddhist consciousness, or the awareness of suffering in the world and diminishing it through open-hearted. The world is empty of meaning. Some paths of Buddhism teach that there is nothing in the world at all. With the idea of two truths, there is also a school that says that there are objects in the universe, but they don't have any meaning. Everything you experience has only the meaning you give it and every time you insist on your meaning being the correct one, you cause suffering. The idea of emptiness subsumes the idea of no separation among people. Bodhicitta says that we are all one in consciousness, that there is only one consciousness, so the idea of one consciousness and the Buddhist teaching of emptiness are manifest together.

Mishlove: And this is Dzogchen or is that separate?

Targ: That would be Mahayana. Mahayana is open-heartedness and emptiness, where the emptiness subsumes open-heartedness. The idea of emptiness implies that there is only one of us. Dzogchen assumes that you've internalized that, and Dzogchen is really, from my view or experience, the fast track for enlightenment, transcendence, or peace. Dzogchen teaches that you have the direct opportunity to experience who you are, which is timeless awareness.

In the 8th century, the great teacher Padmasambhava brought Buddhism to Tibet and wrote a book that seems very contemporary called *Self-Liberation Through Seeing with Naked Awareness*. It reads like a remote viewing book because it says that as you quiet your mind, you discover that you're not principally a physical being, but who you are is naked awareness.

Mishlove: This brings up a much larger issue. I've known you for many decades, Russell. I think of you as a very sensitive, humanistic person, obviously a deep student of Buddhism and other esoteric traditions. How comfortable were you working for the CIA and for military intelligence all these years? Do you think it's really an appropriate home for parapsychology research?

Targ: No, it's not an appropriate home for parapsychology research. It was a good opportunity at the time. I had research I wanted to do, so I sought them out. This is 1972. I had already built a PK electron beam device that you don't know anything about. A person, through this device, with his mind could move an electron beam on a galvanometer. I built my four-choice ESP teaching machine. It's still available from the Apple store at no charge, the *ESP Trainer*. I had, really, a lifetime of doing experiments in this field.

Mishlove: And working with hardware.

Targ: That's right. I was ready to bet my career that I could show people how to do this. I was fifteen years into lasers, a senior scientist doing laser stuff. I told my wife—we had three little children and a house in Palo Alto—"I'm going to do something different now, other than laser work. I'm going to start an ESP program." I was completely confident it was going to work, from my life experience. If you say, "What made you think it was going to work?" My answer is, I knew it was going to work. In a certain sense, why would it not work?

Mishlove: It sounds like you knew it was going to work much in the same way that Pat Price knew he was going to die.

Targ: That's right. Now, Buddhism is not a religion. Buddhism offers you a group of tenets and practices that allow you to control your mind. For example, it gives you contact with the off switch when you're trying to meditate. What do you do when the chatter won't go away? What do you do when you think you're suffering, or overcome with unhappiness? Buddhism gives you a group of things to do to modulate the way you experience your life and the world. Buddhists have, for millennia, been aware you can: quiet your mind, see into the distance, see into the future, heal the sick, [and] communicate with deceased people. It's written about at great length. The first person who talked about this subject, at any length, was the Buddhist Dharma master Padmasambhava in the 8th century. He wrote a very nice book called *Self-Liberation Through Seeing with Naked Awareness*.

Mishlove: He's the one who brought Buddhism to Tibet, as you said.

Targ: Exactly. He's a historical person. He's the one who said, "Your nature is timeless awareness." You're not really made of steak and potatoes. Your nature is timeless awareness. If you quiet your mind, you can expand your awareness into timeless realms. For example, he said,

"If you want to expand your mind, you have to give up your desire to grasp, and to name what you're seeing." In the 8th century, instructors were saying, "Don't try to name the object." That's an analytical error and has been understood for 1,200 years.

There's this famous guidebook of Padmasambhava, *Self-Liberation Through Seeing with Naked Awareness*. That whole book is a guidebook on how to quiet your mind and see into naked awareness. This is a very famous handbook written in 800 CE. Padmasambhava is a historical character. The king of Tibet invited Padmasambhava to come to Tibet, to teach Buddhism as a unifying religion. Without Padmasambhava, there would be no Tibetan Buddhism. Buddhism today is not a religion. There's no deity—this is Russ Targ, physicist speaking. When Padmasambhava went to Tibet, his writing was full of religious symbolism from India at that time, and that was what was taught until the 1200s AD, when Longchen Rabjam, Longchenpa, really purged Buddhism from the deities and taught it like a physics course. It reminds me of Jerry Jampolsky, who's a physician friend of mine, friend of *A Course in Miracles*. He loved *A Course in Miracles*, but he was a Jewish teacher. He couldn't stand all the Jesus mentions, so he just purged *A Course in Miracles* of all the Jesus teaching, and he wrote a famous book.

Mishlove: *Love is Letting Go of Fear.*

Targ: He wrote *Love is Letting Go of Fear,* a hugely popular teaching of a sort of sanitized *Course in Miracles*, much as Longchenpa's famous book called *The Basic Space of Phenomena*, which sounds like a physics text, but it's really a meditation text. It's about Buddhism without deities, which is the way it is today.

Mishlove: I gather then that the message you'd like to leave with people is that if they explore this area, they can maintain a scientific, rational approach and still open themselves up to what we could think of as non-local or metaphysical reality, that these things are compatible.

Targ: That's right. Longchen Rabjam in the 12th century has written sort of—I'll annoy a lot of Buddhists—but he sort of gives you a mathematical treatise on Buddhism: how to quiet your mind, what's there, what's available, [and] what you can do. He's the one who said, amazingly, you are free from the ordinary idea of cause and effect, because your awareness is outside of time. You're not limited by cause and effect: a very amazing thing for somebody to say in the 12th century. His name is Longchen Rabjam, and his friends called him Longchenpa.

Mishlove: Earlier at the beginning of our interview, Russell, you mentioned you had been practicing Dzogchen meditation. I guess Dzogchen is a style of Tibetan Buddhism. You had also implied that you'd been doing that since before you began your work at SRI, or am I mistaken about that?

Targ: I may have said that. I began Dzogchen Buddhism about the same time. I had been a longtime meditator. I was a child Theosophist. So, I was hanging out at the New York Theosophical Society as a graduate student in 1956. I was doing kundalini meditation for a long time, until I decided that it was very dangerous. But I pursued kundalini for quite a while, until I had a scary experience. Not something to be done without a teacher. So, I was an experienced meditator by the time I got to SRI.

And the teachings of Longchen Rabjam came to be published at the turn of this century. For a long time, these teachings were considered secret. The Buddhists didn't want to release them because who knows what could happen if they got into the wrong hands. Then, eventually, the powers that be or the Dalai Lama, or whoever decides these things, decided that his writings, which are so difficult to read, are self-secret. That is, you could put *The Basic Space of Phenomena*—which is the book that I first read by Rabjam—you could put that on the newsstand and not a person in a thousand would be able to make [either] head or tail of the book.

As it turns out, that book is really like a transmission. I read it at a time when I didn't know anything about Dzogchen Buddhism. I finished the book thinking, "That's a remarkable book. It's self-evidently true." Of course, there [were] some things we didn't quite understand, but a decade later, when I reread the book, I realized it was a transmission. The Lama who introduces the book says, "Simply having this book in your library is enough for you to receive the transmission of this remarkable volume." I think that's what I experienced when I first read it twenty years ago. So, it was really twenty years ago that I got into Dzogchen Buddhism as a student and a practitioner.

Mishlove: You describe that as the fastest path to enlightenment.

Targ: It's a path that doesn't involve rules of behavior. What Longchenpa assumes is that your life is on an even keel having solved the mundane problems, and you're trying to learn what to do with your consciousness. He has quite a few books that I would call "mind training" that are transcendentally clear, and what I think of as self-evidently clear.

I came across this slim volume, *The Basic Space of Phenomena*, years before I was really prepared to read it. My daughter was very ill, and she gave me that book. I read that while she was with a teacher named Gangaji. At the time, I didn't know who Longchenpa was, but it's as though I was channeling this book because I found it so self-evidently clear. On the jacket flap, the lama who introduced the book wrote, "This book is of such spiritual power that you don't even need to read it. Simply having it on the shelf of your library will communicate the essence of the teaching."

Mishlove: If I recall the story as you explained it to me, the book was given to you by your daughter Elisabeth [1960-2002], a friend of mine who was dying at the time. She went in to have a final session with her spiritual teacher, Gangaji, before her death, and, while you were waiting, you read that book.

Targ: Gangaji was my teacher at the time and taught Advaita. She is an American woman, a contemporary teacher, and was inspired by the teachings of Ramana Maharshi.

Russell Targ with Gangaji, 2014.

Mishlove: Part of that lineage, you might say.

Targ: Yeah, definitely. Sit down and meditate on the question, "who am I", and discover your transcendent nature of being one with nature and the universe, which is identical with what Longchen Rabjan and many others would teach.

Helena Blavatsky, as the great founder of Theosophy, taught that the religious or the metaphysical aspect of Theosophy is that we have direct access to nature through our consciousness. Her students were able to parse the nature of a hydrogen atom through pure meditation over a block of paraffin.

Mishlove: You also mentioned the same idea comes through in the philosophy of Spinoza.

Targ: Spinoza was a pantheist. Fortunately, he was Jewish so he wasn't burned at the stake, but he was excommunicated.

Mishlove: It's the only example I'm aware of a Jew being excommunicated.

Targ: He thought that the divine was in all of nature, and that was available to you. The idea of non-duality has been with us in written form since the time of the Buddha and throughout science, philosophy, physics, and metaphysics, a good 2,500-year lifespan. The idea is that, to a greater degree, experiencing your life without duality is a way of experiencing your life without suffering.

Mishlove: In your career, in particular, through the work of remote viewing, you have found that you can take ordinary people who don't have any mystical proclivities—soldiers, CIA contract monitors, business people—and ask them to concentrate on some unknown target that might be located anywhere in space or in time, and that, statistically speaking, they're able to do this with a very high degree, in your experience, of replicability.

Targ: "Concentrate" probably wouldn't be the right term. I told them to simply quiet their minds and tell me about the surprising images. It is more of an acceptance than a concentration.

Mishlove: Allow.

Targ: I managed to gain support for our program, in many cases, by meeting with some government bureaucrat, including right up to the Undersecretary of Defense, who wanted to see something psychic by saying, "Just sit down, we'll show you how to do it. You don't have to believe. It has nothing to do with belief. Your adjutant has gone off with my colleague someplace, and I have no idea where they are. Just tell me what you're experiencing. Just what surprising images come into your awareness."

Mishlove: You've seen this happen repeatedly.

Targ: It's really permission-giving rather than teaching.

Mishlove: I think this is a very clear-cut empirical demonstration of the philosophy of non-duality.

Targ: I certainly think so. It's coherent with timeless awareness because it's no harder to describe an event or an object in the distance than it is to describe it from across the street. And it's no harder to describe something days or weeks in the future than it is to describe a contemporary thing. Your consciousness has access to time and space.

Mishlove: Russell Targ, thank you so much for sharing these important insights with me and with our audience.

Targ: Thank you very much for the opportunity.

7

The Life, Death, and Afterlife of Elisabeth Targ

Recorded on March 3, 2017

Jeffrey Mishlove: Today we are going to celebrate the life of Dr. Elisabeth Targ, a pioneer researcher in the field of psychic healing and the daughter of my guest, Russell Targ. Welcome, Russell.

Russell Targ: Thank you. I'm happy to be here. It's always embarrassing to hear you say all these books with "mind" in their titles and say the author is a physicist. How did that happen?

Mishlove: How did it happen? Well, we talked about that in an earlier interview. One of the most fascinating aspects of your life, so much so that it was the subject of an editorial by the renowned skeptic, Martin Gardner, is the influence that you had on your daughter, Elisabeth [1961-2002]. I remember her as a teenager tagging along with you at meetings of the Parapsychology Research Group in San Francisco that you co-founded. We watched her grow up and become a successful psychiatrist, perhaps the most successful researcher in the field of psychic healing before she tragically died.

Jeffrey Mishlove interviewing Elisabeth Targ in 2000 for the original *Thinking Allowed* television series.

Targ: It was a tragedy. In that article, Martin Gardner called us three generations of troublemakers, because it started with my father who was the publisher who brought Erich Von Däniken to the United States. He found Von Däniken in a book stall on the Seine in Paris and looked at his manuscript. My father had a lifelong interest in science fiction, so he published Von Däniken's book, which greatly stimulated my interest in science fiction, magic, and extrasensory perception. He also published a biography of Helena Petrovna Blavatsky, the occult princess.

Mishlove: And the biography of Eileen Garrett.

Targ: Gardner said it started with William Targ and included his son Russell, a blind parapsychologist, and his daughter Elisabeth, who was a psychiatrist doing psychic healing. Gardner couldn't stand it.

Mishlove: Not only was she a talented researcher, but she worked with you in remote viewing experiments, and participated in a well-known experiment doing remote viewing between the Soviet Union and the United States.

Targ: We visited Djuna Devatashvili [1949-2015] in 1983 when I was a guest of the Soviet Academy of Sciences. Elisabeth, who was a Russian translator, among other things, interviewed Djuna, in Russian as Djuna described where our partner was hiding in San Francisco, 6,000 miles away. That was a very successful experiment. It was judged by a blinded committee and was found to be highly statistically significant. Djuna described all sorts of interesting things like an animal with pointy ears and glass eyes, a building with slanted sides and a flat roof, and some kind of plaza near the water. The traveler was at the merry-go-round at Fisherman's Wharf in San Francisco, exactly as Djuna described.

Mishlove: Elisabeth shared with you this sense of certitude. She knew from an early age about the reality of psychic functioning. I don't think she ever doubted it, from my knowledge of her, and that made her, like you, a successful researcher.

Targ: Oh, she never doubted it at all. We expected her to describe what was in her birthday presents before she opened them when she was a child. From an early age, her psychic functioning was taken for granted.

Mishlove: Let me ask you this, though, was this necessarily the case with your other children, or was she different in that regard?

Targ: I remember doing an experiment with my son. I'd come home with a very unusual object from SRI that I had purchased for use as a target object. I asked my son, Alexander, "Can you guess what's in this box? What do you visualize?" He said, "It's very funny, there's a cylinder with holes in it, but I don't know what you would put in there." It was a Saturday Night Special revolver, which, in fact, does have a cylinder with six holes in it. I thought that was very crisp. He just looked at the wooden box, and those are the words that came to him.

Mishlove: So, your other children did exhibit psychic ability.

Targ: Everybody had permission and an expectation to be psychic.

Mishlove: Would it be the case that every parent was that way, frankly. Let's talk about her research.

Targ: When she graduated from medical school, she began working at the California Pacific Medical Center [CPMC] as a psychiatrist seeing patients and doing research involving distant healing. She wanted to know if various healers around the country—energy healers, religious healers, Native Americans—could send their healing intentions or their energy. Barbara Brennan worked with energy healers.

Elisabeth was treating AIDS patients in 1998, just past the peak of the AIDS epidemic in San Francisco. She created two groups of patients with thirty in each group. The patients knew what the experiment was, but they didn't know which group they were in. In fact, neither did she, because the patients were chosen at random by someone else and [were] a careful, double-blind, but balanced choice of patients.

The chosen healers from across America were given pictures of these patients. Each healer had quite a few people that they were sending energy to. During perhaps twelve weeks, Elisabeth saw the patients every week, and recorded how they were doing. At the end of twelve weeks, the patients were analyzed, one with respect to the other, and then it was decoded, [and] the blind was broken. It was found that the people in the healing group, the people for whom prayer was said, had significantly better outcomes than the control group.

Mishlove: Across several dimensions.

Targ: They found that the test group required fewer trips and fewer days in the hospital, had better psychological scores, and better self-esteem. It was a highly successful study, published with no problem in the *Western Medical Journal*.

Mishlove: She did other studies after this as well, didn't she?

Targ: She then did a study involving glioblastoma with patients.

Mishlove: A very serious, deadly brain tumor.

Targ: The AIDS patients were already on the healing triple-drug cocktail, and they were not as sick as she expected them to be.

Mishlove: Because, already, medicine had made a lot of progress with AIDS treatment.

Targ: It sounds unkind to say that they weren't sick enough, but it was easy for the discernment of the statistics to show that the group receiving the spiritual energy did much better than the controls. The glioblastoma patients were much sicker, and, a couple of months into the study, for unknown reasons, Elisabeth was diagnosed with glioblastoma and died within a few months after that. There was, at that time, no treatment for glioblastoma. There is now a palliative treatment that allows you to live a year, or a year and a half, but there was no such thing for Elisabeth.

Mishlove: No, she was only in her forties.

Targ: She was forty years old. She had not reached forty-one.

Mishlove: It was a very tragic death, and very ironic that she would contract glioblastoma, which is not contagious.

Targ: No, of course not.

Mishlove: At the very time she was researching it. Here is Elisabeth doing state-of-the-art work in psychic healing, [and] getting it published in mainstream medical journals.

Targ: Not many of those.

Mishlove: Yeah.

Targ: Not many people doing that.

Mishlove: No, it's very unusual, and her work was first-rate. It was being endorsed by one of the major medical centers in the San Francisco Bay Area.

Targ: Randolph Byrd at San Francisco General Hospital, and Lewis Harris, another cardiologist at Washington University Hospital, at about that same time, had published studies involving their cardiac patients. Lewis Harris had 600 patients, and Randolph Byrd had 300 patients. In both those studies, the postoperative recovery was much improved in the patients receiving spiritual prayers or energy from other people. What's interesting is that their study was just as significant as Elisabeth's study, even though she had fewer people, because the effect size of her study was so much greater.

Mishlove: Perhaps, like you, she had a certain ability as an experimenter, too. I guess the word to use would be "psi-conducive", because psychic functioning seemed to work well around her.

Targ: It certainly was. She was a very psi-conducive experimenter.

Mishlove: Then when she died very suddenly, very tragically, I remember it well, and was very touched by it, as were all of her friends.

Targ: I remember sitting on the terrace at the house where I lived and where she died, in Portola Valley with my son, Nicholas, and her husband, Mark, and we started talking about Elisabeth. She was such a powerful character that we wondered if we would hear from her. At that point, all the lights went off, and then came back on. It was a relatively new house, and I'd never seen all the lights flash, as though somebody pulled the main circuit breaker, then they went off and on again.

Mishlove: One more time.

Targ: Yes. We took that as a signal that she's still with us in some sense.

Mishlove: We talked in an earlier interview about F. W. H. Myers, Frederic Myers, a psychical researcher from the 19th century who made many appearances through mediums after his death. Certainly, given Elisabeth's lifelong interest in parapsychology, it would make sense that she would want to communicate if that were possible.

Targ: Indeed, she seems to have done that.

Mishlove: I had heard many stories from different people, including her ex-husband and your former co-author Jane Katra about these appearances and many physical manifestations. I had a vivid, lucid dream about her in which she came to me. We were friends, so it wouldn't be unusual that that would happen. I said to her, "Elisabeth, how nice to see you. I've heard such wonderful things about your communications, and especially the physical manifestations." At that moment, I was awakened from my dream because the phone right next to my bed was ringing. I picked it up, but there was nothing but white noise or static on the other end of the phone.

Targ: It's an unusual phenomenon.

Mishlove: The event was consistent with the many reports found in the two books, *Telephone Calls from the Dead* and *Phone Calls from the Dead*, which was co-authored by my cousin, D. Scott Rogo, along with Raymond Bayless. So there's an extensive history of this kind of communication.

Targ: The night that she died, I was awakened by the impression that my bedroom was flooded with light. I opened my eyes, and I saw everything with crystal clarity. I did not see Elisabeth, but it's as though somebody had turned on the lights in my room. Four years prior to Elisabeth's death, her mother, Joan Targ, had died and I was in my bedroom going to sleep. The phone rang, and when I picked it up there was just static.

Mishlove: You had an experience similar to mine.

Targ: Yes. I've never picked up the phone to hear only static, except in that instance.

Mishlove: I'd have to say the same thing.

Targ: So it must be a telephone system for recently departed people.

Mishlove: Some of my readers may be interested in my interview with Professor Stafford Betty on Instrumental Transcommunication [ITC], in which we go into greater depth, because it's a large field of study. There are thousands of amateurs around the world endeavoring to establish forms of electronic communication with the deceased, and many, many tales of this sort.

Targ: I have seen that. Elisabeth had identified herself, at an early age, as being a remarkable person. Even in nursery school, she was extremely facile at learning foreign languages. When she was eight years old, we let her go to Switzerland to stay with some Swiss friends of ours who had children. She spent about five or six months in Basel attending a school where they spoke German. We didn't realize that was going to happen. When she came back, my father met her at the airport in New York City, and said, "My God, she hardly speaks English anymore." A few years later, she was in Palo Alto High School where she had skipped a couple of grades. The high school students were given a chance to shadow Stanford professors to see what they might like to do as adults. Elisabeth chose Karl Pribram, who was known as a pioneering psychiatrist interested in the holographic brain.

Mishlove: Yes. In fact, some of our readers, if they dig around a little bit, will come across my interview with Pribram.

Targ: Elisabeth was quite tall, and well spoken so Pribram mistook her for a college student.

Mishlove: She was twelve at the time.

Targ: He said, "Can you read German?" He needed someone to translate. She hadn't read technical papers, but she spoke fluent German from her time in Basel. She wound up spending several weeks, if not months, translating German technical papers for Pribram. I think that he never caught on that she was a twelve-year-old.

She graduated high school when she was fifteen, and we sent her to a twelve-week summer school at University of California, Santa Cruz, to study Russian, which she was interested in. Midway through that class we met with her teacher who asked if we spoke Russian at home. We said, "Not at all." He said, "She's speaking Russian in a proficient colloquial way, the way elderly Russians do." At the end of twelve weeks, she was ready to go to Russia, which she did a couple of years later.

Mishlove: Extremely precocious.

Targ: Yes.

Mishlove: I can tell you something about Elisabeth that's very relevant that you probably don't know if you don't mind.

Targ: All right.

Mishlove: To do so, I need to share with our readers that you, within the last week to ten days, went through a life-changing experience. You nearly died.

Targ: That's right.

Mishlove: You were in the hospital. You now have a pacemaker.

Targ: I do, indeed.

Mishlove: They thought if they tried to take you to your normal hospital, Kaiser Hospital, you might die before you got there.

Targ: That's what they told me.

Mishlove: Yeah. So, they rushed you...

Targ: I said, "I don't belong to Stanford. I belong to Kaiser." And they said, "You're not going to live that long."

Mishlove: They managed to get you to Stanford University Hospital, and you went through an emergency procedure.

Targ: It was very impressive. I was somewhat anesthetized, but my impression was that the ambulance drove directly to the emergency room, and they took me right into surgery.

Mishlove: They had called in advance, so they were expecting you. This is a major trauma for anybody to go through. Now, here you are, healthy and vibrant and with me, and I'm delighted. About a week before that happened, you heard from your former writing partner and friend, Jane Katra. She had a dream; she was concerned about your health and warned you about it. What Jane didn't want to tell you, but she told me subsequently, Russell, is that she felt that Elisabeth had contacted her and told her to reach out to you.

Targ: That's very interesting.

Mishlove: It's as if Elisabeth is still watching out for you.

Targ: Jane certainly had sent me an email, saying she's concerned about my health. I sent her back a short note saying, I'm doing fine, thanks for your note. Three days later, I was on a gurney.

Mishlove: Jane felt that if she had mentioned Elisabeth at that instance, it wouldn't have been the right time.

Targ: No, that would not have been helpful. Shortly after Elisabeth died, I got a call from her husband, Mark Comings, who said, "I had a strange phone call from a nurse in Seattle who was in Elisabeth's distant healing program." The nurse told Mark that she had a very clear dream from Elisabeth. This was perhaps two weeks after Elisabeth's dream...

Mishlove: After Elisabeth died.

Targ: The nurse told Mark, "I have a call from Elisabeth. She has a message for you." Mark said, "What's the message?" She said, "I don't know, because it's in Russian!" Mark said, "Do you speak Russian?" And she said, "No, I don't speak Russian at all. But Elisabeth insisted that it be in Russian, so she gave me the message one syllable at a time. I'll send you a letter."

Mark called me when he got the letter and asked if I could make any sense out of it. I do speak a little Russian, but not much. I looked at this letter, and there were four little syllables, and then four more syllables, one underneath the other. The top group said in Russian, "I see you." The bottom group said something like, "I adore you." It was the kind of thing that Elisabeth would do. She could have said, "Call my husband and tell him I love him." That would be what an ordinary person would do.

Mishlove: A typical mediumistic communication.

Targ: And nobody would have believed it. It took a really dedicated, focused person to parse this Russian into something that her friend would take the trouble to write down and then send out.

Mishlove: To communicate through a medium; that's quite extraordinary.

Targ: It would be very hard to say that that's super-psi. Skeptics or parapsychologists who don't accept survival say that it's super-telepathy or super-clairvoyance.

Mishlove: Which is impressive in and of itself.

Targ: There's no handle here for the non-Russian speaking woman to parse two Russian sentences into English. So I find that a particularly convincing event.

Mishlove: I know that there are probably dozens of other stories like this that are centered around communications from Elisabeth, and I hope someday to pull them together and do an interview or a program just on that. But one of the things that comes through that people have told me is that not only are these communications evidential, but so is that experience of light. That oftentimes, when Elisabeth manifests from the other side, people feel an overpowering sense of love.

Targ: They certainly do. Jane Katra had another experience if I have time to tell you this.

Mishlove: We'll take the time.

Targ: Jane was applying to be a professor of Health Education at Duke University.

Mishlove: Co-author with you of *The Heart of the Mind.*

Targ: She had a meeting with the chairman of the department and his nursing associate. As they sat at a little table in the professor's office the nurse, who was also a professor, said, "Do you know a woman who died recently, a tall woman with long, dark hair?" Jane said, "As a matter of fact, I do." The nurse said, "I wouldn't normally interfere with a meeting like this. Do you mind? But this deceased person is very insistent that you give a message to her father, because the message that she wants to communicate will convince him of her survival. She's been unsuccessful so far. Remind him that when I was a little child, he and another person forcefully stuffed me into a red dress against my will, and it was a traumatic experience for me. If you tell him that, he will know that I survived."

Jane communicated that to me, and indeed, no other living person knows that I was involved in such a stupid activity. My mother, who was a very society-driven person in New York, had sent a beautiful handmade dress to us for Elisabeth who was two years old at the time.

My mother was making her first trip to California to visit us, and she thought it would be nice if I dressed up Elisabeth to meet her at the airport. My mother was a publicist, so this was her idea to create a little tableau. My wife wore only trousers of various kinds, fashionably, appropriately dressed, but never wore dresses so Elisabeth was having no part of wearing a dress. We finally succeeded stuffing her into the dress against her will, and as soon as we were ready to get in the car, she ripped it off and we never saw it again.

We had no idea that that was a trauma, but Jane's story served its purpose because the red dress was unknown to anyone else other than my wife and I and Elisabeth. Elisabeth was our first child, and we simply didn't know any better. But there is no other source than Elisabeth for this story.

Mishlove: That's the event that convinced you, a laser physicist, of the reality of survival of consciousness.

Targ: That's right.

Mishlove: Russell Targ, what a pleasure to have this time with you and to be able to share these memories of your wonderful daughter.

Targ: Thank you very much.

8

Historical Highlights of Parapsychology

Recorded on July 16, 2017

Jeffrey Mishlove: We'll be exploring the history of psychical research and parapsychology. With me is Russell Targ. Welcome, Russell.

Russell Targ: Good afternoon.

Mishlove: It's a pleasure to be with you. I'm aware that you, in your career as a parapsychologist, have achieved an enormous amount of fame and notoriety.

Targ: Those often go together, don't they?

Mishlove: You've been on the front page of the *Wall Street Journal.* You've published in *Nature* and in the *Journal of the Electrical Engineers Society.* Yet, despite all of this, many people, particularly the critics of this work, aren't aware that the research into this area goes back about 130 years or so. There's an enormous database of work that preceded the good work that you did, and that your work is consistent with this larger database.

Targ: The British Society for Psychical Research with F. W. Myers and the other great researchers began in 1882.

Mishlove: I should mention as well, one of the contributions you've made to the field is to publish the *Studies in Consciousness* series of a dozen of these classical old books to keep that research and that database alive in people's minds.

Targ: Yes. As I was writing my books—new books are always formed from old books if you're writing non-fiction—I discovered that many of the sources I was interested in were either out-of-print, hard to find, very expensive, or all those things. My father was a publisher when I was a child, so I had the idea to make a deal with a publisher that I would write introductions or a preface for these fine old books if they would bring them back into print. We have a dozen of these books together with a couple of new books. They're now available as print-on-demand books for a small amount of money.

Mishlove: You mentioned Frederic Myers, who was one of the founders of the Society for Psychical Research and his classic book, for which you asked me to write the introduction of the Russell Targ edition, of *Human Personality and Its Survival After Death*. That book was initially published in 1903, as I recall, and in 2003 the British Psychological Association had a centennial commemoration of that book because they regarded it as a very important contribution to mainstream psychology.

Targ: What we released is an abridged version. I think the original was perhaps 1,200 pages.

Mishlove: Two volumes.

Targ: This volume is probably 500 pages, and it has the earliest descriptions of Myers' sittings with mediums giving him information about deceased people.

Russell Targ edition of *Human Personality and its Survival of Bodily Death*. Interpretive introduction by Jeffrey Mishlove, 2001.

He was aware that a medium might be using telepathic communication instead. If Myers wanted to know about his friend Joe, who had died many years ago, the medium would most conveniently go into his mind. The evidence for telepathy is much stronger than the evidence for survival.

Mishlove: A counter-hypothesis.

Targ: Myers used proxy sitters such as his servant, and the servant would say to the medium, "I have, in this envelope, the name of a friend of my master, F. W. Myers, and we would like to know what you can tell us." The medium would then tell a story. One of the stories that I like was about Myers' friend who had visited him in North Africa. The medium described a seaside cafe where Myers and his friend were observing the people sitting on the beach. Myers had admired his sword cane, which was fashionable at the time. It looks like a cane, but a rapier would come out of the bottom if a weapon was needed. The friend said through the medium, "That was a fancy of mine just hearing that such a thing

117

existed. I'm deceased now, so I have no need of this. If you still want my sword cane, you could go to my mother's house to the back of the closet. Tell her that I said you could have it." He did go to the mother's house and found the cane, and she gave it to him. The transcript read like a long-distance phone call from the dead, that the medium and the deceased man were having. Since Myers was not there, there was no ostensible source of that information, other than the deceased person talking through the medium.

Mishlove: That is if we consider telepathy to be a short-distance phenomenon. Myers was still alive at the time, so there could have been telepathy at a greater distance, I suppose. His work is remembered for many reasons. As I recall, early in the twentieth century, the Smithsonian Institute magazine published a summary of research that had been done by the Society for Psychical Research. They concluded that we can't say for sure that the psychical researchers have proven the existence of survival after death, but beyond a doubt they've proven the existence of what they then called thought transference, or telepathy.

Targ: That's right.

Mishlove: That was accepted beyond question well over 100 years ago, and yet today it is controversial for reasons that I think are not related to the quality of the data.

Targ: Why isn't survival accepted based on all the many books that there are?

Mishlove: Thought transference, or telepathy, is still controversial and it shouldn't be.

Targ: The skeptics of survival say the evidence for mind-to-mind communication is very strong, but regarding survival, maybe it's a kind of super ESP.

Mishlove: People are afraid because we all want to survive, so could we be deluding ourselves?

Targ: You were saying maybe the medium was reading the mind of the absent Myers. Even if the servant didn't mention Myers, the medium could read the mind of the servant and know that his master's name was Myers.

Mishlove: It's quite a stretch.

Targ: I think it's a stretch.

Mishlove: At least it's logically possible. The interesting thing about Myers is that after he died, he seemed to continue his research from the other side. You've published the writings of H.F. Saltmarsh, who evaluated the "cross correspondences."

Targ: Rudyard Kipling's daughter, who was living in India, a medium in America and a medium in England were all getting these cryptic messages from Myers. Myers was a known poet and a great scholar, so these messages were sent to the Society for Psychical Research in England, where they were then put together like pieces of a jigsaw puzzle. Together, they made a coherent story, a piece of a poem, or a reference to past research and became the so-called cross correspondences.

Mishlove: Many people today have a hard time with this body of information because Myers was a great scholar of classical Greek and Latin, and a poet as well. The messages contain allusions to this literature, but people today aren't as well versed in Greek and Latin as they were 120 years ago. It goes over the heads of a lot of people now. But Myers thought it through very carefully, apparently from the other side. What better way to convince people that he was still alive in consciousness, even after the death of his body?

Targ: That's right. If people don't believe you when you're living, you must do the experiment posthumously. Myers did that excellently.

As I was preparing to talk with you, I thought that I would talk about, perhaps, the famous experiments done by the English medium, Mrs. Leonard. She conducted a séance with F.W. Myers, and Myers talked to his deceased friend from Cambridge, another philosopher. They chatted with each other as though they were spouting philosophy, while one was present and the other deceased. There's a great body of data—to my mind, that's like xenoglossy. It's as though they are speaking a different language, that you can't fake! I've seen the transcript of Myers talking to his friend. I find it very compelling because Mrs. Leonard was not an educated person, particularly.

Mishlove: Another fascinating aspect of the history of parapsychology and psychical research is work that comes out of the former Soviet Union. You published the volume about Leonid Vasiliev performing experiments in distant mental influence.

Targ: Vasiliev was a biologist, hypnotist, and researcher in the 1930s. One of the things that he discovered, and the subject of this book, was mental suggestion or hypnosis at a distance. He was interested to see whether it is electromagnetic. He would put one of his subjects in an electrically shielded room, made of two portions that were sealed together with a mercury trough. As a scientist, I've worked in screened rooms using no mercury, because mercury is a poison. I think of these poor Russian women nodding off to sleep while being poisoned with mercury vapor coming out of the trough and Vasiliev, safely off in another laboratory. He used a random schedule to tell the test subjects when to squeeze a little bulb, which put a mark on a chart recorder. Periodically, the person would squeeze the bulb, and then Vasiliev would send them a telepathic message to go to sleep. Now, as I say that, it's not clear to me how distant hypnosis would be different from telepathy...

Mishlove: No, I think it is a form of telepathy.

Targ: So, the women would stop squeezing the bulb and he would mark the chart when he sent them the message.

Mishlove: What he demonstrated is that it was not an electromagnetic phenomenon.

Targ: The point was it worked just fine in a shielded room because he was able to send them the psychic hypnotic message from a distance. It's a very well recorded simple experiment. He would mark his paper on a random basis when he told them to stop squeezing the bulb. Then they would resume it. This was carried out several blocks away where he was working in Leningrad. They could be in their home and communicate by telephone. Then he did a series between Leningrad and Sevastopol with one of his assistants. It was a 2,000-mile experiment, and that experiment replicated quite well. It's really a long-distance behavior modification. The Russians loved behavior modification. At Stanford Research Institute we were interested in inflowing pictures from a distance. What The Russians were interested in [was] affecting the behavior of people, right up to including distance strangulation.

Mishlove: Well, there's a good deal of evidence that that's just as possible as remote viewing.

Targ: That's right. William Braud, a great friend of yours and mine, did a lot of experiments where the thoughts of one person affect the physiology of another person. In fact, he wrote a book I helped publish, *Distant Mental Influence.* He describes twelve of his favorite experiments. Braud would sit in the laboratory while someone else is in a studio. Braud looks at the person's video image, and, on a random schedule, would try to excite the distant person or relax them. It's quite systematically demonstrated. When Braud tries to excite the subject, their heart rate or their galvanic skin response will increase. When he tries to relax them, he puts them to sleep. Often Braud worked with Marilyn Schlitz, the energetic young researcher. In general, Marilyn had the job of exciting the subjects and waking them up. Braud had the job of putting them to sleep, at a distance, and was very successful.

He published many experiments. I helped him put those together. We chose our twelve favorite published experiments, where the mind of a distant person can directly affect the physiology of a distant person in a laboratory from whom he's very well shielded. I consider that—again we can talk about falsifiability or not—I'm convinced from those experiments, consciousness is efficacious in doing stuff.

Mishlove: One might say it's the basis of psychic healing.

Targ: The thoughts of one person can affect the physiology of a distant person.

Mishlove: It raises the question of whether healing is a telepathic phenomenon, like sending mental or hypnotic suggestions at a distance, or whether it's an energetic phenomenon. We might think of it as psychokinesis on a living system.

Targ: Many healers simply send what I think of as a psychic get well card. They don't need to know what's the matter with the person. And that seems to be surprisingly efficacious.

Mishlove: One of the other books that you published is intriguing to me: *Mental Radio* by Upton Sinclair, who was a well-known novelist in the 1930s.

Targ: And muckraker.

Mishlove: And a muckraker. He was the one who exposed all of the ugliness going on in the meatpacking industry.

Targ: Like the terrible stockyards in Chicago where I grew up.

Mishlove: He managed to get Albert Einstein to write an introduction to one of the editions of that book, *Mental Radio.* Einstein was very impressed with Upton Sinclair's descriptions of what is now called remote viewing.

Targ: Because they both lived in Princeton, Einstein was able to come and see how this worked. Sinclair's wife, Mary Craig, who was ill, was oftentimes confined to her bed downstairs and Sinclair would be upstairs in his office where he wrote his books. He would, from time to time, choose an image from a magazine, or he would draw a simple picture. At two o'clock, Mary Craig would make a drawing of what Sinclair had drawn or chosen on his desk. *Mental Radio* was his collection of the several hundred pictures. Some were excellent, and some were pretty good. There were very few misses comparing what he had in his office with what she drew in her bed.

They resemble the pictures that are shown in another book by French engineer René Warcollier, called *Mind to Mind*. He was interested in understanding mental telepathy and mind-to-mind communication. His big contribution was the discovery that psychic functioning is a non-analytic ability. He found that people cannot get alphabets and numbers. There is a particular kind of distortion that appears. For example, if you have a picture of an American flag as a target object, the subject in another room might draw a couple of stripes and a couple of stars but could rarely put together a complicated object like that which is akin to reading. You can see a pipe, a horse, a sailboat, a dipper, a house, or all manner of things like that, but it's very hard to put together something that has only analytical significance.

Mishlove: Some people have used the holograph as a way of explaining how this kind of perception works. If I understand it rightly, the idea is that every holograph contains some aspect of the whole image. If we are holographs of the universe, then we contain within ourselves some information from everywhere in the universe.

Targ: A hologram can be viewed like a sheet of stamps and if you break off one stamp, you still have the whole picture. Or if you break off a corner of a big matzah, it's clear that it's still matzah.

Mishlove: A matzah is a Jewish cracker.

Targ: As the piece of hologram gets smaller and smaller, you lose resolution. A hologram is usually on a glass plate, like three by five or five by seven inches. When breaking off the corner of the image you still see the whole American flag but at somewhat reduced resolution. There are fewer pixels in the little image than you have in the big image.

Mishlove: It does seem as if that might be an applicable way of thinking about remote viewing.

Targ: In that you tune into the hologram.

Mishlove: That may be why it's hard to resolve, let's say, the American flag, to render it perfectly. Although, occasionally, I know you have seen perfect architectural style drawings of targets.

Targ: I once did an experiment with Peter Hurkos, along with a big group of people, from the parapsychology group that I had. Someone brought us a hologram all wrapped up in black paper. I remember, I was horrified when Hurkos picked this thing up and started to bend it, you could hear the glass breaking. He said, "I don't know what this is, but it's full of energy." It was a picture of an atomic bomb blast. He got the idea of energy, even though there wasn't much left of the picture after he got done exercising it.

Mishlove: That's a funny story. Peter Hurkos was, in his day, a very well known psychic.

Targ: Yes.

Mishlove: We could go on and on about contributions that have been made over the decades. Many of them are quite striking. And yet, they get embroiled in controversy and often get forgotten. I think that's quite a shame, because one of the important things, going all the way back to Frederic Myers, is that the psychical researchers of the nineteenth century, developed very rigorous methodologies.

Targ: They certainly did. One of the books that we didn't mention is a book by Stanley Krippner called *Dream Telepathy*.

Mishlove: I've had the privilege of interviewing Stanley. He was sitting right there in that very chair [talking] about that book. It's a classic.

Targ: You want to tell us?

Mishlove: The Maimonides Dream Laboratory in Brooklyn, New York, back in the 1960s, conducted the first work where people were put to sleep and then awakened when the EEG readings showed rapid eye movements. They were asked to report their dreams. Meanwhile, in distant locations, other people were attempting to send them mental imagery. They used independent judges, a double-blind protocol and found that the dreams did indeed, statistically, significantly replicate the imagery that was being sent to them. While that research, like all research in parapsychology, gets mired in the objections of scoffers who refuse to accept it, this work has withstood the test of time.

Targ: One of the series of experiments in the new edition of that book talks about psychic Malcolm Bessent who would go to sleep each night and then asked to dream about what would happen to him the next morning. They would wake him up during his rapid eye movement sleep and ask him about his dream. And, he might say, "I'm dreaming about being very cold. I'm shivering. I just feel overcome with cold and there's something blue that's making me cold." The next day, using a random number generator, they would go through their list of 100 different events. For that day, they put his feet in ice water and blew cold air on him with two blue electric fans. He dreamt about that treatment six hours earlier before it was even chosen. Precognitive dreams are the most common psychic experience that people have even though the idea of getting information from the future is the least understood of psychic phenomena.

Mishlove: Russell, I know we have barely scratched the surface of the vast history of parapsychology and psychical research, but I hope this conversation will stimulate our readers to go to the library and dig into this wonderful literature for themselves. Thank you so much for being with me.

Targ: Thank you.

9

Successful Military Intelligence Applications of Psi

Recorded on July 26, 2017

Jeffrey Mishlove: Today, we'll be exploring some of the successes in applied parapsychology that emerged from the remote viewing research program at SRI International. With me is Russell Targ, the co-founder of that program. Russell is a laser physicist and is also the author of many books on parapsychology, including most recently *The Reality of ESP: A Physicist's Proof of Psychic Ability.* Some of his other titles include *Mind at Large, Mind-Reach, The Mind Race, The Heart of the Mind*, and *Limitless Mind.* Welcome, Russell.

Russell Targ: Happy to be with you, Jeffrey.

Mishlove: It's a pleasure to be with you. You know, it's so funny to me that people are debating, even parapsychologists, whether ESP really exists. In your career, you have seen repeatedly that it does exist, that it can be highly accurate at times, and that it has very real practical applications. Frankly, that's why the U.S. government funded that remote viewing research program, year after year for two decades.

Targ: You're right; parapsychologists are as skeptical as anyone. More than once, when I've lectured at the Parapsychological Association meeting, talking about some of the very successful experimental work we did at SRI, I would say, "Of all you researchers, who is absolutely convinced that something like ESP is real?" And I might get two raised hands. Stephan Schwartz might put up his hand, Ed May might put up his hand …

Mishlove: I would.

Targ: All the other hundreds of people say, "Well, there may be some error, can't tell, looks like it's ESP." But there are really a very small handful of people who, after decades of work, are still willing to stand up and say, "Lasers exist, streetcars exist, ESP exists."

Mishlove: I think some of them are honestly afraid they'll get fired from their jobs if they come out too strongly.

Targ: It's about fear.

Mishlove: At one point, you learned that the CIA felt that you were too much of an enthusiast.

Targ: They could trust Hal Puthoff to be a company man, but they couldn't trust me because I was enthusiastic about the reality of the phenomena that they had given us $20 million to investigate.

Mishlove: Let's talk about some of the reasons for your enthusiasm.

Targ: We could talk about how this program at SRI went on for twenty-three years at a rate of about $20 million to support the program, so the CIA evidently thought we were doing something worthwhile.

Mishlove: We're talking maybe about a million dollars a year, which is peanuts for the CIA.

Targ: It's peanuts for the CIA, but quite a bit of money for an ESP program.

Mishlove: Absolutely. Probably the most significant funding for ESP research in the history of the world.

Targ: If you look in the newspapers, you don't see anything about ESP anymore. Psychic abilities were real when there was a well-funded program at SRI and when there was money on the table. When the money dried up, people weren't sure anymore.

Mishlove: For all we know, there is money going into programs that are simply not disclosed to the public. Given all the controversy surrounding the field, maybe that's wise, because on top of the irrational skeptics you often have people who believe for religious reasons that ESP is real enough but is the work of the devil.

Targ: If you're interested in ESP, the easiest way to pursue it would be in the secret basement of the CIA. Why else would they cancel a program that was working so well?

Mishlove: Of course, people will ponder that question for a long time, and I've heard many different answers, but let's share some of the real success stories.

Targ: An early example was during the Iran hostage crisis, in 1980. Hostages from the American embassy in Tehran had been captured by the so-called dissident students. We were visited by Jake Stewart, who was a naval captain for the Office of Naval Research, gave us a picture in an envelope. I had no idea it was a picture of a hostage. He said, "Can you tell us about this person?" I went into our little shielded workroom with a psychic of the day, and I said, "I've got a picture here from Captain Stewart, I have no idea who it is, could be Khrushchev, could be the president, could be anybody. Tell me about this person." The psychic held it and rubbed his hands over the envelope and said, "This person is very sick. This is a man who's in a dark place, both physically and mentally. He seems to be shaking, but I see him getting out of that place. I see him coming out of this darkness into the light, and he's getting on an airplane." I gave that information to Jake Stewart who said, "I'll see how you did."

Mishlove: You often did not get feedback working with the government agencies.

Targ: Within a week we learned that it was Ambassador Richard Queen [1951-2002], who was the deputy American ambassador to Iran, and had developed multiple sclerosis when he was in captivity. The Iranians agreed to release him because they didn't want an American to die in captivity, and he was flown to Germany for medical care. Everything that the psychic had to say was correct, with no input at all, just to tell me about the picture in the envelope. That was evidence of the kind of things that mediums often do in so-called cold readings, where you ask about a person who will often be deceased. But in this case, the psychic was able to give quite a good rendition of the health and the circumstances of this live person.

Mishlove: You didn't get feedback, I presume, so you don't know whether that reading was at all instrumental in facilitating the release.

Targ: No, I don't think it was instrumental. I think that at the time that we were doing the reading, the Americans were working with the Iranians to get Queen out of the cell that he was in. I just don't know if it's true. But certainly, the description was appropriate for the contemporaneous situation.

Mishlove: When you're dealing in an area like military intelligence, you've got the issue of accuracy or inaccuracy, but you also have the issue of actionability, whether, even if the information is accurate, is it useful?

Targ: This scenario may have been a test for us because the fellow was in a dynamic situation. He wasn't somebody who'd been in jail for 50 years, but he was somebody who was sick and they hoped to free him. So, there was some action associated with the task.

Mishlove: There are many other examples I know of that involved highly accurate and important information that was retrieved through remote viewing.

Targ: We made a deal with the CIA to spend half of our time doing research into how psychic abilities and remote viewing operated. As physicists, we wanted to know whether ESP degrades with electric shielding and found that it does not. Also, whether it is affected by distance or time. The most important thing we discovered is the non-local nature of the ability, that the accuracy and reliability was independent of distance and time up to a few days or weeks into the future.

One of the operational targets we had from the CIA was in 1974, when our contract monitor Ken Kress came to us with a slip of paper and said, "We want to know what's at this place, and what's going on?" I, of course, had no idea at all. It could be any place on the planet; it could be the inside of the Pentagon; it could be anything.

Mishlove: Was it a coordinate or a number?

Targ: It was geographical coordinates. I worked with Pat Price [1918-1975], the retired Burbank police commissioner, who said that he had done psychic stuff like this all his life. As a police commissioner, he would hear a crime being committed in the city of Burbank and send the squad car to where he saw a frightened man. They would arrest the perpetrator on the spot. He came to us with a scrapbook showing his psychic exploits as a police commissioner.

Price and I went into our little shielded phone booth with a table where we did our work. Price began to draw a complex R&D facility. He said, "There is a very big gantry crane rolling back and forth over a building. I'm going to have to draw that." It appeared to be a very big gantry crane because he drew a little man coming up to the wheel and it had an A-shape. He said, "I'm lying in the sun; the sun feels good, and, as I'm lying on this building, a giant gantry crane is rolling back and forth over my body."

Pat Price's remote viewing drawing of Russian gantry crane. The large size is established by the tiny man standing by one of the wheels.

CIA Initiated Remote Viewing

UNCLASSIFIED

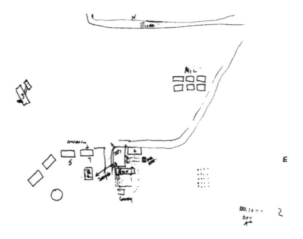

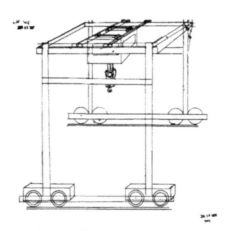

UNCLASSIFIED

CIA drawing of the Russian gantry crane based on satellite photos.

We delivered Pat's drawing to the motel where Ken Kress was staying with his partner. They looked at it, and then at one another. Out of his suitcase, he took a secret carrying case and unrolled this drawing. They didn't want us to see the photograph because that would reveal the resolution of their cameras. In the middle of that drawing, there was this giant gantry crane with eight wheels, four on either side of the building, rolling on tracks. This surprised even us though we were two years into a successful remote viewing program.

Mishlove: This was during the Cold War era and a target site that turned out to be in the Soviet Union.

Targ: In Soviet Siberia. There was no way for us to cheat. I was with Price in the shielded room and the contract monitors were testing us. Price would have had no opportunity to find out what the target was, nor could he find friends to break into the CIA vault to find out what was at those coordinates. The coordinates alone wouldn't show you anything because satellite photography was just being developed. The monitors said, "Well, that's remarkable. Can you tell us what's going on in that building?"

So, Price and I went back into our shielded room, and he told me, "They're building something out of steel gores. I see men in white coats there." A gore is like a flat orange segment. He said, "This is like a 60-foot diameter sphere that they're making." So, he drew shell-shaped gores totaling, 60 feet in diameter. He said, "This is very thick steel; they're having trouble welding it together." We took that back to Ken Kress and said, "This is what's going on." He said, "Well, that's very interesting."

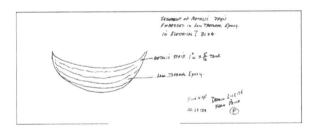

Pat Price's illustration of a metal gore.

Price died before we ever got feedback about that event. Two years went by before satellites caught these big spheres outside of that building. *Aviation Week* published pictures of the 60-foot steel spheres, 58-foot steel spheres, and mentioned they were having trouble welding them because the steel was so thick.

Giant Russian steel sphere with gores. From Pat Price 1974 remote viewing. First published in *Aviation Week*, 1977.

Price described something that was utterly unknown to the CIA at the time. We didn't even get credit for this remarkable remote viewing because no one knew about it until two years later. Eventually, that viewing did go into Ken Kress's detailed write-up of psychic research during the Cold War.

Mishlove: The CIA wisely regarded this simply as another form of intelligence input.

Targ: They don't trust just one—you need more than one asset to give you the information. They knew that the crane was correct, because they had a satellite photograph of it strongly matching what Price had drawn but they had no corroboration for the gores making up the steel sphere until two years later.

Mishlove: Was he able to talk about the purpose?

Targ: He thought that it was a containment vehicle vessel for a nuclear weapon. We were later told that it was a containment vessel for a particle beam weapon. Even today, different people have different ideas of what they're used for. I think that the Soviets built big steel spheres for a number of purposes. I've heard authoritatively two entirely different answers from different people. The spheres were described correctly, and they are made of gores. My mother taught me that a woman's flared dress would be a four-gored skirt. But until Price said the word, forty years later, I hadn't heard the word gore.

Mishlove: Well, now our readers know. I think one of the most impressive instances had to do with the discovery—when Joe McMoneagle was the remote viewer—of a new class of submarine that was completely unknown to the U.S. government at the time.

Targ: I interviewed six Army intelligence people, and they were the basis for creating a psychic Army Corps at Fort Meade. One of the principal remote viewers was Joe McMoneagle. One day, Skip Atwater, the director of the Fort Meade remote viewing program, came to Joe, a contract monitor, and an interviewer and said, "Can you two guys figure out what the Russians are doing at these coordinates?" Joe said, "I see them welding, a lot of welding going on. They're making a submarine." Joe was an intelligence officer, so he would recognize a submarine if he saw one. He said, "This is the biggest submarine I've ever seen. In fact, this is more than 50 percent bigger than any submarine I've ever seen."

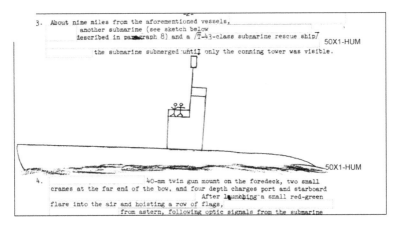

Joe McMoneagle's remote viewing sketch of Russian submarine.

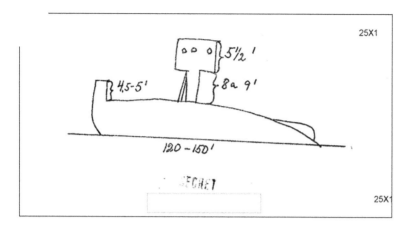

Joe McMoneagle's remote viewing sketch of Russian submarine.

Joe McMoneagle's remote viewing sketch of Russian submarine.

It turned out to be twice as big as any submarine he had ever seen. He used his hands in the interview to describe that it was like two hulls welded together and had new capabilities, including forward-firing missile tubes, so they could fire nuclear weapons while they were underway. He drew pictures of the sub and said, "I think this is going to be released 120 days from now." It was released in 114 days. That was the first anyone on the American side knew anything about this supergiant submarine, the Typhoon-class sub. You can now look on the Internet and see Typhoon-class submarines that are extra-wide, looking surprisingly like a whale floating in the ocean.

Russian Typhoon class submarine.

Joe described that with no input at all, except the coordinates of a building that was a quarter mile from the ocean, so it even didn't seem likely that they would build a giant submarine there. It turned out they had to then get bulldozers and backhoes and cut a channel from the building to the sea to release the sub.

Mishlove: That's quite interesting.

Targ: We have Joe's drawings of that; contemporaneous drawings.

Mishlove: That would seem to be a significant breakthrough and an almost perfect example, I should think, of the sort of thing that the CIA would be very, very pleased to get.

Targ: The director of the CIA, Robert Gates said at the time, "That's a remarkable drawing. It was really your lucky day today."

Mishlove: Russell Targ, it's ironic that we should close on such a note. Obviously, people who would like to see parapsychology pursued more have a lot of work to do yet. But we can all feel very proud of what has been accomplished up until now, and particularly by yourself and your colleagues. Thank you so much for being with me.

Targ: Thank you.

10

Mind and Matter

Recorded on November 8, 2018

Jeffrey Mishlove: Today we'll be exploring the mind-body relationship in the light of parapsychology and ancient spiritual traditions, as well as philosophy. With me today is Russell Targ, physicist, and parapsychologist.

Hello Russell, it's good to be with you once again. Today we're going to talk about the mind-matter relationship. I know you approach the topic both as a parapsychologist and as a physicist. I suppose it's worth mentioning the founders of quantum physics, and particularly Erwin Schrödinger, wrote extensively about this, and when you read their writing, it reads rather like the writings of various mystics.

Russell Targ: That's right. Schrödinger was an enthusiastic Vedantist. Advaita Vedanta was something that informed his whole life, and the idea of Advaita means not divided. Advaita in Sanskrit means no division. The push throughout all the teachings from Ramana Maharshi through the present teachers—Ramana Maharshi was an Advaita teacher in the 1950s—and the idea of Advaita and their whole view of consciousness is that we should make an effort to discover who we are. You could sit with an Advaita teacher, as I have for a decade. My teacher was named Gangaji. She was a student of Ramana Maharshi's student, F.W. Punja. I have a picture of Punja with Gangaji and a picture of Gangaji with me, so I feel that I'm part of that lineage. Obviously, I'm not a teacher of Advaita Vedanta. Gangaji greatly informed me and calmed me down for the decade that I was with her.

Now, this is an unusual situation with you and me, Jeffrey. I've spoken to you several times about interesting things I've seen in the laboratory. I can describe what happened, what we think it means, and what the data looks like. I am what I think of as a reformed positivist, logical positivist. The positivists feel that if you can't verify and quantify what you're describing, it is nonsense. So, from the beginning of the 1900s, where you had Bertrand Russell, and Moritz Schlick, and Wittgenstein, and Kurt Gödel, all these famous guys were passionate about the problems that religion created.

Mishlove: You're talking about the Vienna Circle, I imagine.

Targ: The Vienna Circle. These are the logical positivists, historically known as some of the smartest people in the world, especially Wittgenstein and Bertrand Russell. They felt religion was a huge problem. Out of their musings together came the idea of logical positivism. Karl Popper was part of the group, and his idea of verifiability: if you can't verify it, it didn't happen.

Mishlove: Actually, Popper focused on falsifiability, as I recall.

Targ: That's right. The mind-body problem was really created in the 17th century by Descartes. Descartes did a lot of very, very useful things. He invented Cartesian coordinates, which is a great contribution. He had this idea: he sees a body in front of him, and there appears to be a mind inside, quite different from the body. He had the idea there is a non-corporeal mind, quite different from the physical body. What's not generally known is the mind-body, first enunciated, in our epoch at least, by René Descartes in the 1600s, created the mind-body situation. He believed in survival, which I had not initially known. I wrote a whole book dealing with the mind-body problem. I never encountered the idea until recently, until preparing for your interview. Descartes' big interest—he felt confident he was going to survive his physical death.

Mishlove: He was, I believe, a devout Catholic.

Targ: Descartes' mind-body dichotomy meant that when they bury him or cremate him, he's not entirely gone. His mind survives.

Mishlove: As I recall, he defined two different substances. Matter, he says, has extension in space, but mind does not have any extension in space.

Targ: That's right. What we know now is the mind is efficacious. He did not know that. If Descartes had known, he may have had a different idea.

Mishlove: The scientific research in parapsychology, of which you've done an abundant quantity, really didn't exist in his day.

Mishlove: That's clear. To me, the question regarding those experiments is: was this effect caused by psychokinesis, by a direct interaction from the mind of one person to the body of another person, or was it more a question of telepathic suggestion, even telepathic hypnotic suggestion, or mind-to-mind?

Targ: I think that's not known, but for our discussion today it doesn't matter. We're showing that consciousness can do stuff at a distance, outside the body. This is the connection.

Mishlove: The philosophical implications of that fact are so staggering, the academic community in general refuses to even look at the data.

Targ: That's right. The people who particularly have trouble with this idea are the materialists. Today, the materialists call themselves physicalists, a kind of apology for promissory materialism. The physicalist says, "Yes, there seems to be something like ESP, but I don't believe that consciousness does stuff. We'll one day know how it all works on an electromagnetic or other basis. I'll promise you one day, the physical phenomena will come out, but of course, right now, there's no evidence for it."

Mishlove: The reason that there's no evidence is because, as I understand it, when we talk about matter in terms of physics, there's no evidence of anything akin to consciousness in molecules and subatomic particles.

Targ: That's right. There's no evidence. There are vitalists who believe that everything is alive; everything is consciousness. I happen to know that Lenin believes that. So, within the Soviet Union, the idea of psychic abilities was okay. Lenin supported Vasiliev, as you know, in the Soviet Union, because Lenin thought that everything had consciousness. He didn't think that it was supernatural.

Mishlove: He was a Marxist materialist, and yet he was open to the idea that material itself possessed consciousness.

Targ: That's right. Wasn't he clever?

Mishlove: Yeah. Today there are people who take a similar point of view. This idea is called panpsychism. Panpsychists would say, there is no difference between mind and matter.

Targ: That's right. Niels Bohr based his whole view of the atom and the wave-particle interaction. That is, wave-particle duality comes from this problem: when you shine light through a prism, it behaves exactly like waves going through glass. They disperse in accordance with their color, precisely as waves would do. So, if you have an examination, saying, I've shone a light into this prism, how far will the red disperse from the blue? You will know how to calculate based on the index of refraction of the prism. For your next question, you'll say, I've shone this light beam through two slits, and get two-slit interference. Based on the distance between the slits, how far will the particles move? That's, again, a wave interaction. Waves interfere.

However, I spent a lot of time in a laser laboratory, where you can start dropping in filters, dropping in neutral density filters. You can cut down the laser intensity on the screen until you know for a fact you never have more than one photon in the system at a time. If you have a photon detector back there, it goes tick, tick, tick each time a photon goes through. But if you have a photographic screen to accumulate all the photons, you'll see the same interference fringes. So, it's very mysterious. There is no satisfactory explanation. A lot of people will tell you stories, and the stories are rather metaphysical.

The story a physics student wants to know is, since you have only one photon in the apparatus at a time, how do you get interference? There's presently no good answer for that. There are things in physics for which there are no good answers. But this thing is a very good demonstration of wave-particle duality. When you shine light through a prism, it's a wave. When you shine light through an interferometer, they're particles.

Mishlove: I'm under the impression, Russell, that one of the reasons people, particularly in academia, are so fixated on the materialistic metaphysics is because of the enormous success we have had with technology. Automobiles, airplanes, computers, atomic bombs are all the result of the application of materialistic science. It seems to me that people make a mistake when they generalize about the great success of technology, when they say, well, this is how nature itself is. Nature conforms in every regard to the principles of materialism. When, as you've pointed out, there are many, many areas of physics that lead to paradoxes.

Targ: That's right. At the end of the 20th century, I was frequently on the stage with Michio Kaku. He did not believe in consciousness at the time. He's a string theory physicist.

Mishlove: He's written extensively on hyperspace, as I recall.

Targ: That's right. He said, within a few years, we will be able to describe everything you can measure in an equation less than an inch long. So, there.

Mishlove: Promissory materialism.

Targ: Right. Within two years, astronomers had discovered dark matter and dark energy. He's completely back to the drawing board. That's happened again and again, century after century.

Mishlove: But, from the perspective of Advaita Vedanta, it suggests that we think of ourselves as ego consciousness; our life history. We're born and we die. But it would seem to me that Advaita suggests we are much like drops in the ocean of a larger consciousness.

Targ: That's right. Advaita was very happy with the drops in the ocean idea. The conclusion of Gödel, which people don't like, is there are many questions you're simply not going to get an answer to because: they don't have an answer in ordinary logic.

Mishlove: The answer must come from outside of whatever logic system you're working with then.

Targ: Or it may be a misapprehension of the space-time you live in. That is, we've become masters of four-dimensional space-time. Four-dimensional space-time does not support a simple explanation of psychic abilities. Psychic abilities transcend ordinary space-time. The evidence is they are non-local. That is, the accuracy and reliability of what we see is independent of distance and independent of time. This precept violates ordinary ideas of relativity and space-time. It would be wrong to say that it violates physics. There are models where physics continues to function with a multidimensional model.

So, if our space-time is complex, rather than just real, you can then postulate eight-dimensional space-time. To keep it simple, we have regular space-time as four dimensions. Each are familiar dimensions: up and down, left, and right, back and forth, are there except, in addition to having a real part, they have an imaginary part. So, the eight-dimensional model isn't adding in new dimensions. I am not saying four dimensions is not enough, so let's add in another dimension. What Elizabeth Rauscher and I have been talking about is a complex space-time, first talked about by [Hermann] Minkowski in the 1900s. Minkowski was a friend of Albert Einstein, who was not able to formulate special relativity even. He could hear the idea, but it didn't work out in ordinary space-time. Minkowski said, if you make one of the dimensions imaginary, x, y, z, space dimensions, and multiply time by the speed of light, and the square root of minus one, giving yourself an imaginary number, then you have a complex space-time. And relativity works, and relativity has been working very well.

What Minkowski had in mind was a totally complex eight-dimensional space-time. Einstein said, I don't need that. Thank you very much for complex time; that'll do the trick. So, our idea of complex space-time is not, here is ESP, let's add another dimension. Maybe it will work, as it has good antecedents from the foundations of general relativity.

Mishlove: What you're describing also reminds me of some work done by Wolfgang Pauli. In his Jungian analysis, he had a series of dreams in which he was encountering, in his dream life, a mysterious figure who was explaining the mind-body problem to him. Basically, he said exactly what you're saying. The imaginary dimensions, those dimensions multiplied by the square root of minus one, an imaginary number, are the dimensions that signify consciousness.

Targ: I think it's the correct picture. So, what we've been talking about is the mind-body problem. We have a lot of evidence that the mind is efficacious, the mind can actually do stuff. But materialists have a problem with the survival of consciousness. My thoughts can send you a picture, that is, I do this trick with attendees when I do workshops., Often I will ask them to do experiments with one another. Simply, visualize something and get your partner to draw what you're visualizing. These are pure telepathy experiments, except, of course, the person eventually gets to see the right answer, if you draw it. In the distance experiments of William Braud and Marilyn Schlitz, there's nothing to see. My thoughts affect your physiology.

Now, we could also talk about the other side of it. The mind-body problem is worried about: is the mind efficacious? I think there's good evidence that it is. There's also good evidence that some aspect of the mind survives.

Mishlove: Let's talk about that, because I know that our good friend Ed May, a parapsychologist who considers himself a physicalist, has often said if we could prove survival of consciousness after death, he would give up physicalism and join one of the other philosophical camps.

Targ: I talked to our good friend, Stephen E. Braude about it. He blew me off saying, "That's interesting, but you don't know any philosophy. We could have a philosophical conversation. Let's just agree that you don't know what you're talking about."

Mishlove: A former chair of the philosophy department at the University of Maryland, so he's quite particular.

Targ: He's a good friend of ours and a distinguished philosopher. My point is that you can't fake being a philosopher any more than you can fake speaking French, if you don't speak French. Instead of going back to those people, I thought I would tell you about a recent case that is probably not known at all, in which I had contact with all the participants. I was giving a lecture in Boulder, Colorado. I was teaching at Naropa Institute, a Buddhist teaching center. Afterwards, I was invited to a party at a beautiful house in Boulder. One of my students approached me there and said, "Could I tell you about an event recently, where someone died and appears to have come back? Would you be interested in such a thing? Because I was there, and it happened."

She's a very nice lady. I think of her as an older woman. Of course, I'm now much older than she was, but she had all this nice fluffy white hair. She was talking about an event that took place with her granddaughter. She ran the League of Women Voters in Arizona, where she lived. So, grandma took her little granddaughter Haley for a walk in the Ozark wilderness area, to visit the waterfall. So, grandma and six-year-old Haley went for a walk down the path with some friends, and they could see the falls in the distance, but it was getting late. Grandma said, we've got to go back. Haley didn't want to do that, and she somehow slipped away. One minute she was there, and, if you've ever walked with a child, you know that children can just disappear.

Mishlove: Yeah. And this is a heavily wooded location?

Targ: That's right. They looked all over, and they couldn't find her. Grandma was panic-stricken. What she said is, "I had this flash that my son would kill me if I lost his daughter. 'Why did you take my daughter to the wilderness?'" So, she quickly went back to town. They returned with a search party. They still couldn't find Haley. Fire trucks came in. A book was later written by a tour guide who lived there. He wrote a book about this incident because the terrain is so rough, he couldn't imagine how a child could get lost and survive. But a day went by, and they had helicopters coming in searching for Haley. So, this was a major event in the Ozark wilderness. This would have been—I met them in 2001, the year the book was written by the tour guide, and the year in which this happened. As it turned out, Haley was found. I got to meet Haley, her grandmother, and the tour guide. Why we're talking about this, by the end of the second day, everyone was frantic. There's this little child in flip-flops. She's on the top of a bluff. The canyon was 700 feet below. It was like a plain at the ridge of the Grand Canyon. One misstep, and you're dead.

She went to a medium living not far away. "I've lost my granddaughter. It's going to be a tragedy. We're in the wilderness area here," she told him. He says, "All right, I understand. I've got a whole picture of the scene in my mind. Just believe me, they're going to find your granddaughter. She's being taken care of by a young woman right now. And tomorrow, two men on horseback will find her. Don't worry about a thing." So that certainly put her mind at rest. She didn't know what to make of this. She's not into psychic stuff, not into dowsing, but she said it certainly put her mind at ease.

The following day, two men on horseback were searching at the base of the falls. There's Haley asleep at the edge of the river, totally okay, except exhausted and a bit emaciated, having nothing to eat much for three days. They took Haley across the saddle and brought her back to town. She was alive [and doing] well. Grandma was there. Haley said, "Everything was fine. As soon as I lost you, a little girl came along. She said she would take care of me. This girl was named Alicia. Wherever we went, she was able to find berries and stuff to eat. We would hide in her cave at night." She was gone for two nights. But Alicia was taking care of her. Alicia had a silver flashlight with her, so they could always see where they were going. "And so here I am, and I'm OK."

She drew a picture of Alicia for grandma, so she could see what this person looks like. Grandma is very alert. This is obviously a crazy situation because Haley was just fine. Who is this woman who took care of Haley, this five-year-old Alicia? Grandma went to the local library and asked an astute question of the staff: has any young person ever died in this area?

Mishlove: In other words, the grandmother suspected that this Alicia was not a living human being.

Targ: That's right because Alicia wasn't there. As soon as the horses came, Alicia disappeared. But indeed, 10 years ago, there had been a cult hiding out in the area. It was a violent cult. The short story is that Alicia had been killed and buried in the area. The father was sent to prison and the mother was sent to prison for a short time. After she was released, she was able to tell her story in the newspaper. Grandma was able to find the mother of the deceased girl, whose name was Alicia. For crazy cult reasons, they had taken away the dolls of this girl and gave her a flashlight from which she was inseparable. So, the living Haley was able to draw a picture of the deceased Alicia in her old clothes, bib top overalls and tied back pigtails. In the book, they show Haley's sketch of the girl who used to live there. She had been dead for 10 years. The book describes what Alicia looked like, how her name was spelled, correctly, and the fact she was attached to this flashlight, because her parents had taken away her dolls and given her the flashlight. So, this is a case that passes a lot of different tests.

Mishlove: Just so that I'm clear about this, the mother also had been in prison for Alicia's murder?

Targ: That's right.

Mishlove: I see.

Targ: She was an accessory. It was a cult. I don't remember what the inside—I don't know why they killed the girl.

Mishlove: But in any case, you suggest that this story is evidential of survival, because the child Alicia, murdered 10 years prior, was still active in spirit form.

Targ: That's the thing that impresses me. She's active, able to initiate activity. First, she helped keep the six-year-old alive. The reason the tour guide got involved is that he was there when the kid was rescued. He said, there's no way. He leads people on careful trips in and out of this area. This is like a day-long hike. A little girl in flip-flops would be in peril of her life to try and do that. He [Tim Ernst] wrote this whole book, *Search for Haley*, trying to figure out how she could have possibly done it without getting killed.

Mishlove: Well, the story surely suggests the existence of a spirit world.

Targ: It shows that certainly something survives.

Mishlove: The idea that such a world could interact with the physical world by virtue of the mathematics of an eight-dimensional space, that you and Elizabeth Rauscher have worked on, makes good sense.

Targ: If somebody survives—there's sort of prima facie evidence that this little girl survived, at least to the extent of doing helpful stuff. Her spirit was efficacious. It's more than just a shadow on the wall.

Mishlove: I would view your model, to the extent that I understand it, as being a dualistic model. There's a separate spirit world, there's a physical world. They interact with each other according to the underlying mathematics of an eight-dimensional space you've described.

I would never say there's a spirit world. I would say, we all reside in an eight-dimensional space. That is, when somebody calls me up on the phone, as happened when I worked at Lockheed—I'd given a talk to a wealthy community in the San Francisco Bay Area. The next day, my hostess called me up. I'm sitting at my screen spreading numbers for the next year, which is my least favorite thing. Because of my bad vision, I hate having to do spreadsheets on the screen. What she wanted to know is, could I help her find something? I said, "Well, possibly." She said, "I lost my diamond tennis bracelet. My husband will kill me if I don't find it." I said, "Well, I don't know what a tennis bracelet is." She explained, it's a beautiful platinum circlet, covered with diamonds, and a present from her husband. She couldn't find it anywhere. She looked everywhere. Could I help her?

So, I just swung my chair away from the video monitor, closed my eyes, and said, "Well, do you have a place on your property where there are two 4x4 uprights with pointy tops? I see these two 4x4s set in the grass." I didn't see her bracelet. I just shared with her the image that came to me. She said, "Well, near the back door of my house, there are two 4x4s to protect the house from people who might run into it with a car." I said, "I don't know what it means, but go take a look by those 4x4s, because they meet my requirements." It's a clear image unrelated to my anxiety or wish fulfillment or preconditions or daily baggage. It's an unasked-for clear image.

She came back from her two 4x4s and said, "I'm so happy. Thank you so much." She did not say the magic words, "How can I help you? Can I give you anything to support your research?" But she was very grateful that I found her bracelet. So, I think that we reside in this eight-space. If you call me up and say, "Will you find something for me?" I don't have to go through a bunch of mumbo jumbo, as any experienced remote viewer would not have to. The space is available. I think we reside there. Longchen Rabjam, a great Buddhist teacher of the 12th century, said, we are timeless awareness. We reside in this timeless space that's available. We're not made of meat and potatoes. If you think what you see in the mirror in the morning is who you are, you're in for a lot of suffering. What Longchen Rabjam said is, you are timeless awareness. Because your consciousness is timeless, there's no cause and effect for consciousness. If you're outside of time, cause and effect doesn't apply. So, you're able to see into the future, as well as in the distance.

I think that the space in which we reside is not—I don't think there's a separate psychic space. As an idealist, I resist the idea of any kind of dualistic thing, dualistic space. I think we reside in the space in which we reside. Our consciousness is just part of awareness. That is, consciousness is not made of meat and potatoes, in a sense, any more than we are. That is, whatever survives, survives in this space-time realm. It coexists with where we ourselves reside.

Mishlove: So, you're identifying yourself as an idealist.

Targ: I would say so. Certainly not a dualist.

Mishlove: Well, Russell Targ, this has been a great conversation.

Targ: I'm a reformed logical positivist now. I no longer think it's necessary to burn the believers.

Mishlove: Well, Russell Targ, it's been a great pleasure talking with you. Thank you so much for being with me.

Targ: Thank you, Jeffrey. I'm glad to share my stories.

11

Third Eye Spies

Recorded on November 12, 2018

Jeffrey Mishlove: Today, we are going to explore *Third Eye Spies.* This is the name of a new documentary produced by my old friend Russell Targ. Russell is the author of many books. He's been on ten previous interviews with me here on the *New Thinking Allowed* channel. He initiated the remote viewing program at SRI (Stanford Research Institute) International, funded by United States Military intelligence organizations. That's what this documentary is about. Welcome, Russell, it's a pleasure to be with you again. Congratulations on the pending release of your documentary. I know you've been working on it for many years. To begin, you could explain to our viewers why you put so much money and time and energy into this film. Why is it important to you?

Russell Targ: I'm happy to be with you, Jeffrey. I'm glad you got a chance to see my film, soon to be released. *Third Eye Spies* describes the work we did during the first decade of our psychic research and psychic spying activities at SRI. We had a 20-year program. I participated in the first decade. Hal Puthoff and I are both laser scientists, and we were involved in getting the program started because of bona fides with the CIA and NASA. I could go into CIA in April of 1972 and say, "I have an idea to teach people how to be psychic." If they had not known me from my earlier laser work, they would have thrown me out. Because I had done work for them before, I could get a hearing with Kit Green, a physician there. He thought the psychic teaching idea was interesting, and in due course, we were able to start a program at SRI. I thought it was important because I spent my whole life doing magic.

I worked for fifteen years as a physicist, even though I knew that one day I would be doing ESP research. I had to get some kind of credentials so that people would give money to pay attention to the SRI project. It's very hard, as we know, for psychologists to get money to do ESP. A lot of people have done it and had difficulty getting financial support. Hal and I were quite successful because NASA and the CIA just thought, this is another program for these physicists. We'll fund them as though they're doing a physics program. The funding amounted to one or two million dollars a year, which is an outrageous amount for anybody trying to do ESP work.

Mishlove: Of course, it's a small amount of money for the government to spend, but a lot of money in parapsychology research. Russell, you've just told me some of your early psychic experiences.

I suppose it is one of the reasons the government was willing to fund the program repeatedly, year after year, because of your credibility as a scientist. It's not as if you come across like some sort of New Age partisan or guru.

Targ: That's true. I never came across as a guru. I think my strength then was [that] I felt no hesitation or doubt that psychic abilities were real. Oftentimes when I attend an ESP conference, people who have spent a lifetime doing research still say things like, "Gee, if ESP were real, then we would see such and such." A distinguished person said that to me on the 100th anniversary of the Society for Psychical Research. An American professor got up and said, "I'm happy to be here celebrating the 100th year of the SPR. If this is ever shown to be true, it'll be very important for all of us." I was ready to punch him in the nose. Many of us have, at this point, spent our lifetimes doing this work.

Mishlove: I think it's part of your unique personality that you have a way of saying "this is real" and people get it. You are such a focused, solid human being, that when you say it's real, it sticks.

Targ: I think it is because I have no doubt in my mind. I'm not pushing my own psychic prowess. I have got a dozen years of experience as an interviewer talking to people, helping them pull out of their subconscious a psychic image as compared with the noise. In engineering terms, you might say ESP is a signal-to-noise problem. I can't help them with their ESP, but I can help them. My experience and discernment can help people tell what's psychic and what is not. You and I had an experience just like that.

Mishlove: That was one of your basic functions in the laboratory, as a monitor of remote viewing experiments.

Targ: I was the interviewer. In this film, the interviewer is really a very appropriate name. I'm not a viewer. I'm between the subject and the target, so I'm sort of an "inter-viewer."

Mishlove: That's an interesting way to put it. In effect, you've got a research subject, a percipient, who was put into a sealed room. In the radio physics laboratory at SRI you had a room that was so tightly sealed, radio signals could not penetrate.

Targ: That's right. We were all locked in with cipher locks, as in the experiment you and I did. I can say anything to you as an interviewer because I have no idea what the target pool is. I've no idea where you might possibly be, and certainly not where the people are hiding on that day.

Mishlove: So your role is to help the percipient, or the viewer, elicit the correct information about the target.

Targ: I can tell you about all sorts of interesting things. We found downed airplanes, Soviet weapon factories, and hostages carried away in Africa. That's all very interesting, and, if you believe me, as many people will, it sounds like an amazing way to spend a decade. In the film, we were able to get the cooperation on camera of our two senior CIA scientists: Kit Green, a physician and head of the Life Science Branch of the CIA; Ken Kress, a PhD physicist, and an operational undercover person eventually given charge to work with Hal and me. Then there was Sidney Gottlieb, the sort of the force behind this. Gottlieb was running the MK-Ultra program. In his mind, we were sort of a subset of MK-Ultra. And, in fact, he wanted me to use LSD to enhance people's psychic abilities.

Mishlove: MK-Ultra, as I recall, goes back to the 1950s and did administer LSD to unsuspecting persons.

Targ: That's right. To scrub out their memories. I told Gottlieb, I'm familiar with LSD, but remote viewing is an intellectual activity. You need your analytical functions to help you separate the signal from the noise. When somebody takes LSD, they're both not interested in doing your silly task, and their analytical functions are, of course, greatly impaired. He understood me. Our good fortune with the film project is that we came along just when all the senior people were retiring. Ken Kress and Kit Green, both formidable, highly respected scientists and CIA agents, come on camera and investigate the lens and say, "Yes, I was there; these things really happened, just the way Targ says." That's priceless. They may or may not believe me. But these two scientists giving heartfelt descriptions of what they saw and how they participated in the experiments, what they believed and what they didn't believe, is really what carries the film.

Mishlove: As I understand it, Russell, the program was initiated by you and Hal Puthoff at SRI International, a major industrial military think tank in Menlo Park, California. But, at some point, a decision was made to open a separate unit within the US Army at Fort Meade, Maryland. Can you describe how this came about?

Targ: Through the whole program, and not really known, is the CIA didn't trust me. We have Ken Kress on film saying, "You were really doing great work in the program. We know you from your laser work, but basically, we didn't trust you. You were too enthusiastic over this stuff, so we were concerned about your credulity." No one ever came to me in my laser lab and said, "We can't give you money because you believe in lasers." That would have been ridiculous. It really was not until we made this film, when Kress would look right at me saying, "You guys did great work. You described the weapons factory, you found the airplane, you found the hostages, but basically, we had to take this away from you because Pat Price was essentially omniscient." He could quiet his mind and describe anything. Price could read hidden objects, and, conceivably, he could psychically see the launch codes to release a nuclear missile.

They were somewhat frightened of Pat Price. Every task they gave him, he could do. He could describe the weapon shop in Russia, what was underground in Russia—what was in the safe at the National Security Agency in Virginia. He was almost 100%—very, very accurate. The CIA has this prime function to keep secrets, and with Price there were no secrets. That really troubled them. So, at the end of one series, when Pat described a giant crane and underground tanks in central Russia, they just took Price away from SRI. The CIA set him up as a functionary, as an operative, in Virginia.

Mishlove: The Fort Meade program developed after that, I presume.

Targ: The Fort Meade program started after they took Price away. In a certain sense, he was too hot to handle. Price was too dangerous to be left to the researchers in California. What they wanted me to do is train up some Army intelligence officers. They could then have them under complete control, as with Price. Hal and I were introduced to a room of thirty Army officers, men and women; mainly men. "Choose six that you can train to be remote viewers." We did that. I chose Joe McMoneagle as one of them.

Mishlove: He became an excellent world-class remote viewer. He still does that work.

Targ: As far as I know, Joe is the most reliable, competent remote viewer in the world today. He was the first one I had the task of training, from this Army group. Of course, I showed lots and lots of people how to do remote viewing before Joe. Joe came in, perhaps, 1978. I was prepared to deal with him. He was my first customer in the US Army program.

Targ: An image came in and you said, "It looks like Macy's." It's as though I was asking you to tell me something in French. You just said something different. I said, "That doesn't sound like French. Why don't we try it again?" This is my strength as an interviewer. I would say, "That simply doesn't sound like remote viewing. Tell me what you are feeling, what else comes to view." I think this process was very helpful in a strict signal-to-noise way. Ingo proposed the idea of analytical overlay and mental noise.

In the recent period, in the 1940s, René Warcollier, the French engineer, wrote a book called *Mind to Mind*. He talks about mental noise and the problems with guessing. He described the issue at some length.

Mishlove: If I may, let me regress. We were talking a little earlier about Pat Price and how the CIA determined to bring him under their own control. Your documentary makes a big issue of the fact that, shortly after he left SRI to work directly with the CIA, he died. His death remains, in your mind at least, something of a mystery.

Targ: That's right. It was a very early experiment at SRI. Kit Green wanted to see if we could penetrate a facility that he had complete control over. He was confident that nobody in our lab at SRI knew anything about this place. In fact, full disclosure, the place he chose was a log cabin built by one of his colleagues in West Virginia. That log cabin was just over the hill, they say, from the Sugar Grove top secret crypto NSA facility, where they used microwave dishes to spy on the Russians. Both Pat Price and Ingo Swann were given the geographical coordinates of the place. Sugar Grove was probably indistinguishable from the log cabin in the coordinates they were given. But both Pat Price and Ingo described the Sugar Grove listening outposts with their big microwave dishes and government buildings. Price went on to describe [how] down in the basement is where the action is. He said, "There's a row of green filing cabinets. I can read the names on the files, and they say something called 'eight ball' and 'rack up' and 'pool cue' and '14 ball,' a whole bunch of file names pertaining to billiards. That's what I get." That's what he saw, together with some other words. I can't remember it all right now. All the files appear in our film, *Third Eye Spies,* where we have the whole list of what Price was able to dig up from Sugar Grove. We gave those to Kit Green. He was shocked because he was looking for a log cabin, but since Pat and Ingo both described the same thing, he thought he could drive up, look at the log cabin and follow the road past the log cabin. There was a guarded gate there. He's CIA, so he knew he could go through the guarded gate. He saw the big dishes the two psychics described. Then he asked inside, at the appropriate security place, "Do you have something here called 'rack up' and 'eight ball' and 'cue ball'?" They're like, "Oh my god!" They were the code names of some top-secret programs down in the files in the basement. Kit Green saw the green filing cabinets there. It's as though Pat Price went to the coordinates. As he described it, from 5,000 feet, he could see the cabin. But who cares about a log cabin? The secretive CIA guys wanted to know about the government facility. Price went into the government facility and into the building through remote viewing. He had total control over what was going on there and was able to read those file names.

As you say, the NSA was angry: not with us so much, but with Kit Green. They wanted to know, why would the CIA have California psychics penetrate a top-secret facility? Don't you know better than that? We had a very acrimonious meeting with the NSA, CIA, and Pat Price at our facility. The NSA guy turned to Pat and said, "If you're so psychic, why didn't you go where the coordinates said?" And he said, "Well, in psychic space, the more attention you have on hiding something, the more it shines like a beacon. Your facility was much more interesting than the log cabin."

Hal Puthoff, Kit Green, Russell Targ, & Pat Price, 1973.

Mishlove: Parenthetically, after all of that happened, Kit Green or others in the CIA decided that they wanted Pat Price to work directly for them rather than with you at SRI?

Targ: Yes. One of the things the CIA discovered, which we point out in the film, was that Pat Price was an enthusiastic Scientologist. He would meet with his auditor each day, after taking part in top-secret activities with Ken Kress. Ken was running Pat Price like an agent. He would say, "What's going on here? What's going on in the Libyan Embassy?" We talk about this in the film. Price described, accurately, where the code room in the Libyan Embassy was, and he was in the code room. He had other information about it, too. Price was a formidable psychic spy beyond what anyone had ever seen before. Each day, after taking part in these top-secret activities, he would tell his Scientology monitor what he and Ken had been doing at the CIA.

This is true, what I've told you. I don't know if the CIA learned of this before the break-in to the Scientology Celebrity Center. I didn't learn about this until two years later. The Celebrity Center was broken into by the Internal Revenue Service because Scientology was not paying taxes, and other things. It was the FBI and IRS who discovered the file there on Pat Price and Ken Kress doing psychic spying. They called Kress, and that's all in the film. Kress describes his horror at discovering not only was his own cover blown, but that Price was revealing all this information to the Scientologists. Now, this is true. I don't know if the CIA discovered this early on. Price was a smart guy and very psychic. He wasn't a trained spy. He was just living in his farmhouse in Virginia. Every day he would meet with his Scientology contact monitor. We know this occurred because we've got the data.

Mishlove: He was a police commissioner, as I recall.

Targ: A police commissioner in the city of Burbank, California. What I conjecture in the film—and I have no proof of this—is since Price was no spy, he wasn't trained in spy craft. He was working for the CIA. He probably got caught in telephonic conversation with the Scientologists, or was overheard or had intercepted mail. Can you imagine? He's only a few miles from CIA headquarters, working with them on top-secret stuff. It seems obvious to me he was surveilled, in some way. It wouldn't make sense if they let this old psychic guy work day after day with no surveillance. I think they discovered, as I put in the film, their Superman was a double agent. He's working for the CIA and working for the Scientologists. That's an insuperable problem. What do you do when you discover Superman is working for the other side?

Mishlove: You seem to imply in the film, this might have been a Russian operation. As I recall, there was some hint about Russian intelligence saying they murdered a psychic.

Targ: Someone told that story to Hal, yes. In the film, I have a conversation with Uri Geller, in a shielded room in his house in England. Geller is a very psychic guy. He worked for Mossad for years. I told him, of course, Pat could have had a heart attack. He had a heart condition. The CIA could have killed him. Or the Russians could have killed him. Those are the three possibilities that come to mind. There might be some fourth undreamed-of possibility. My guess is, it was most likely the CIA or Russians. I have no first-hand, excellent information to allow me to decide.

The truth is, five months after leaving SRI, the most psychic man in the world mysteriously died. He knew he was going to die because he said goodbye to a lot of people. He bought a million-dollar life insurance policy for his wife, at the airport as he was leaving home. He changed his plans to make sure he visited his son in Salt Lake City before he came to visit with us at SRI. He then later died in Las Vegas. So, Price was aware his life was in danger.

Mishlove: I can imagine that Pat Price's death gave you pause to reflect on the appropriateness of the work you were doing, bringing parapsychology into the intelligence community.

Targ: In my recent book, *The Reality of ESP*, I quote from the Buddhist tome, *The Flower Ornament Scripture*. It's a big Buddhist book written in the time of Christ. Among other things, it spells out all the different things available to the prepared, quiet mind. The idea of practicing high-level functioning of psychic ability is identified and spelled out. You are expected to have this ability. You're not expected to take it to Las Vegas or to spy for the CIA. You're expected to include the elements of a broader awareness—timeless awareness—into your life. I feel in a certain sense, ESP is what it is. It's available.

I didn't do anything unethical. We didn't kill any people or spy on any people at SRI, who didn't want to be spied on. I kept my ethics intact. We took money from nefarious people to do some research. It wouldn't have gotten done otherwise. This can be an apology or, I could be fooling myself. Everything we did, the great preponderance of it, is now revealed. and there's never been any stinking fish pulled out: "How could you guys have done such a terrible thing?" There is no such terrible thing. We found General Dozier, kidnapped by the Red Brigade. We reported on Richard Queen, captured by the Iranians, and described his health, where he was, and that he would be released because he was so sick. We did a lot of amazing things.

The head of Naval Intelligence came to us and said, "We have a picture of a person in this envelope. Can you tell me what his situation is?" It was a sealed envelope. I sat down with the psychic in our little shielded phone booth. He said, "It's dark where the guy is. He's very sick. He's having trouble moving. I see him leaving the place and getting on an airplane very soon." It took all of fifteen minutes to locate Queen, describe his situation, and describe what was going to happen. I think working for the CIA is certainly problematic. I realize they're a nefarious organization and have killed a lot of people through MK Ultra. We didn't do that. They say in the stock market, "... money is fungible." As people financed us to do what we thought was interesting, we published our findings in *Nature,* in the Proceedings of the Radio Engineers, and the American Institute of Physics. We published our work in first-rate, prestigious, American, worldwide organizations. The parts that were secret have now been revealed. Partly, as I got interested in this film, I went back to the CIA, under Freedom of Information. I got a vast quantity of historic material released. There are now 70,000 documents since I first asked for clearance. I would say, in answer to your question, in all of the 70,000 documents, there was never a smoking gun for a terrible action we made.

Mishlove: As I recall, you left that program in the early 1980s and went on to do some other very interesting work after that. The military intelligence involvement continued for more than a decade after you left the SRI program. It was eventually disbanded. As far as we know today, there's no public information available, of any government-sponsored parapsychological activity, certainly not at the applied level. How do you think remote viewing will evolve into the future?

Targ: In the film, we talk to Kit Green. He assumes the program is still going on. Of the people who came to look at our program from the CIA, two of them turned out to be excellent remote viewers. This film is remarkable. We had many, many hours of interviewing with both Ken Kress and Kit Green. We got a chance to spend several days interviewing Ken, for example, and learned that people I trained up, a man and a woman, very good remote viewers with me, went back to the CIA. Then began doing remote viewing with Pat Price. They had a little remote viewing book club on the side, doing this stuff. Since remote viewing works so well, it would be absurd, in a certain sense, for the CIA not to be doing it. In the film, Ken Kress states [that] some high-level people told him the program is still going on, in the basement of the CIA. That would make sense.

Mishlove: It would make sense. I suppose it might be a good thing. Overall, for viewers of your new documentary and for viewers of this *New Thinking Allowed* series, who might wish to pursue their own remote viewing abilities, working with the CIA is probably not in the cards.

Targ: No, that would not be ideal. In my book, *The Reality of ESP*, I have a chapter telling you how to work with a friend. I don't tell you how to find a friend, but assuming you have a friend, you could work with another to do remote viewing trials. Much like we did at SRI while learning to separate the signal from the noise. In our film, *Third Eye Spies*, we show people doing remote viewing on camera with very great success. In fact, the *third eye* is part of Hindu tradition. 2,500 years ago, in the *Yoga Sutras of Patanjali*, he mentions it. In the chapter called "Powers," he describes looking into the distance, looking into the future, healing the sick, and diagnosing illnesses as part of your meditation. He says, "Don't get hung up on psychic abilities. Psychic abilities could be a stumbling block toward your own transcendence and spiritual development. It's out there, so I'll give you a chapter on what psychic abilities are like." That's 2,500 years ago. This subject was very well understood then.

Mishlove: The third eye itself, I believe, refers to the *ajna* chakra, located right about here [middle of forehead], which is thought to be an organ of psychic sensitivity.

Targ: It's thought to be the pineal gland. We don't know if that's true. There is no evidence at all that it's true, but that is what the Hindus believe. Their meditation, the *samyama* meditation, is to quiet your mind. In Patanjali's writing, it's as though you're developing the psychic muscle; you're developing your pineal gland, and it allows you to become more psychic. I have no reason to believe that this is true, except he was right about a lot of other things.

Mishlove: There's fascinating lore concerning the pineal gland.

Targ: Our best remote viewers have been meditators, in general. Remote viewers, who weren't doing meditation initially, became meditators because they thought that it was helpful.

Mishlove: Surely, for anybody who is on a spiritual path, meditation is a very good thing to learn. Along the way, almost anybody on a spiritual path is going to open in some way or another to various, what parapsychologists call, psi abilities.

Targ: That's right. When I was first a graduate student at Columbia, I got involved with the Theosophical Society in New York. I was twenty years old. I learned about this organization [that was] interested in psychic stuff. They had a beautiful home in midtown Manhattan. They frequently had lectures on fairies, psychic abilities, and the ancient wisdoms. You were encouraged to separate the good from the bad, the useful from the non-useful. Helena Blavatsky had a new spin on the Vedic tradition.

Mishlove: That's fascinating. Of course, the Theosophical Society is a very important organization in terms of the evolution of the whole consciousness movement and what has come to be known as New Age culture. It strikes me that the fundamental message of your documentary is that remote viewing is an ability available to virtually everybody.

Targ: It's available to anybody. Some people are better than others. Our nature is timeless awareness. You can expand your awareness into timeless realms. This is an ability we have. This is taught throughout Dzogchen Buddhism. All the Dzogchen teachers agree: you can learn to do this as part of your nature. The reason I sort of dwell back and forth between what was going on 2,500 years ago [and now] is, I want to emphasize that psychic abilities are not New Age. This isn't weird stuff just developed in the 1980s.

Mishlove: Russell Targ, it's been a pleasure talking to you. I wish your documentary a very successful run.

Targ: Thank you, Jeffrey. It's been a great pleasure to talk with you.

12

The Strength and Reliability of Remote Viewing

Recorded on September 23, 2019

Jeffrey Mishlove: Today we'll be exploring the reliability and strength of remote viewing. My guest is Russell Targ, the author of *The Reality of ESP: A Physicist's Proof of Psychic Abilities.* Also, *Limitless Mind: A Guide to Remote Viewing and Transformation of Consciousness.* He co-authored two books with Jane Katra called *Miracles of Mind* and *The Heart of the Mind.* He co-authored a book with J.J. Hurtak called *The End of Suffering.* He co-authored a book with Hal Puthoff called *Mind-Reach,* with an introduction by the great anthropologist Margaret Mead. He co-authored *The Mind Race* with Keith Harary. Russell has also written an autobiography called *Do You See What I See?* and produced the video documentary, *Third Eye Spies.* Welcome, Russell. It's a pleasure to be with you, once again.

Russell Targ: I'm very happy to have a chance to chat with you, too.

Mishlove: I know we've had many conversations, but this one I think is especially important because within the parapsychology community there are some who are skeptical of the strength and reliability of psi, and remote viewing. There are still parapsychologists who, after decades, are unwilling to commit to the idea that psi exists.

Targ: That's very amazing. It's true. Ten years ago, I received an award in Paris for my career in parapsychology. I talked about the work we did at SRI (Stanford Research Institute) and a decade of remarkable events. Then I said, "By the way, of the hundred people here, is there anybody here who is convinced that something like ESP exists?" Three hands went up out of a hundred, and I said, "Why have you guys spent your lifetime doing this if you're not convinced ESP exists?"

What had occurred to me later, as I was thinking about talking to you, is that psychic ability is like radioactivity, from a physicist's point of view. As a graduate student I was working on atomic physics, and I might tell you that, from my studies, radioactivity is really a very powerful ingredient. We should all know about it because it's important and powerful. You might say, "Well, I've heard about that, and I went out into my backyard and shoveled a whole ton of uranium oxide into my basement, and my house is as cold as ever! That radioactivity doesn't do a thing."

I think that psychic abilities are like that. There are certain things you can do with psychic abilities, like find a Russian submarine or a downed airplane or your friend hiding a mile away. What you cannot do is read the serial number on a dollar bill. So, if your criterion for psychic ability is that you've got to read the serial number on the dollar bill, then you're right, ESP doesn't work. I think that the people who are dubious about the existence of psychic abilities have heard amazing things. They just don't know what to do with it.

Mishlove: I think that's true. There are certainly a handful or more of researchers in the parapsychology community who get consistently positive results. You're such a person. We can name others and, in fact, people with whom we're generally associated: Charlie Tart, Dean Radin, and there are others.

Targ: Stephan Schwartz.

Mishlove: It's sort of a mystery to me why some researchers are so successful, and others are not. You would think that, over time, the ones who are not successful—like John Beloff was known as an unsuccessful parapsychologist throughout his career—you'd think he might have learned a few tricks and gotten better if it was a question of learning tricks. Maybe there's something deeper involved—past lives?

Targ: Yeah, I think it's probably harder to be psychic in Edinburgh. It's not known to be a psychic community.

Mishlove: And yet the Scottish people are well known for what they call second sight. In the hills around Edinburgh, there are probably lots of psychic people.

Targ: That's true. Maybe it's being a philosopher or an analytic philosopher because he was certainly passionate about psychic abilities. John Beloff was not a skeptic. He was an interested researcher. He just didn't have any success. I think people who have been successful in parapsychology are often experiencers.

Mishlove: Russell, one of the things that you point out is that at SRI [Stanford Research Institute], in the remote viewing studies you did, you often served as monitor. The role of the monitor hasn't been really studied or appreciated very much. You point to examples of your intuition, knowing just what kind of questions to ask a remote viewer while they're in the process of viewing. It seemed to make a difference.

Targ: Yes, what I learned is that, first, you should be kind to your viewer and not pretend that they're a rat [that] you're running through a maze. You want to treat them respectfully. Your job, analytically, is to avoid any guessing. If we're doing an experiment where my partner is hidden somewhere in the Bay Area, the great tendency [is] to say, "I see where he is, he's at Macy's," or, "He's at the mall," or [in] some other place. My job as an interviewer is to say respectfully, "Let's start that over. Don't guess what you think it is. Just tell me about your experience." Getting people to give up guessing and grasping is a very important element. This is not a New Age idea.

Mishlove: Let me ask you Russell, when did you start studying these ancient scriptures with all their references to things like timeless awareness?

Targ: I was reading the Theosophist materials and about Kundalini meditation in my early twenties. I was a graduate student and my first trip to the Theosophical Society was to hear a lecture on Bridey Murphy: a case of ostensible reincarnation. That would have been 1954. I have a long history with [the] Theosophical Society.

I was a meditator before I got involved with remote viewing. I had a pretty good idea on how to quiet the mental chatter and I tried to set a stage, so people were able to do it, too. I spent ten years sitting in the dark. It's as though the CIA paid for my spiritual development by providing a dark place and a routine for me to sit in the dark half a day for a decade, which is what I did. I helped people develop their psychic ability. I began to have a sense for what remote viewing sounds like. If the person is telling me about their experience, I would encourage them. When they began to drift off into what they think this is, or what it reminds them of, I would try to take a break or have them make a drawing. Even with the people I worked with a lot, like Hella Hammid, I could sense her change of voice, indicating to me that she's in the frame of mind where she gets remarkable remote viewing.

Mishlove: So it would seem as if you had an instinctive, an intuitive sense about, for example, that people shouldn't try to name things. The idea of the "grasping" mentality interfering with remote viewing—somehow you had a natural handle on those things.

Targ: That's right. I get a lot of email. People want to take training with me. As I said, I don't do training. I've done a lot of workshops at Esalen, where we have a nice time. Basically, I am just showing people the moves. I'm giving them permission to make use of an ability they already have. For example, my former wife, who has now died, was Joan Fischer. Her brother was Bobby Fischer, [chess] champion of the world. People were very excited. Well, Joan taught Bobby how to play when they were children. Was she a great chess player? The answer is: Joan had no interest in chess at all. Her job was just to teach her eight-year-old brother, [to] show him the moves. As they say, the rest is history. My job was to show Joe McMoneagle the moves. He had never done this before but all I had to do was set the stage; tell him that his Colonel is hiding somewhere. Then ask him to tell me about the surprising images associated with the viewing. He drew an architecturally correct drawing of the Stanford Art Museum, a strikingly accurate picture. This was his first ever remote viewing. My job is not teaching remote viewing, but sort of setting the stage. And then saying it's okay and here's how you do it.

I had a housemate once who was a spiritual healer. She was practicing intuitive diagnosis for clients. She said, "Well, I could teach you to do that," and I said, "Oh, good." So, she said, "I'll come over and write the name of a person on a card." I said, "No, no, write three people's names on three cards, and when you come, we'll shuffle them up. Because if I'm sitting across from you describing somebody, I don't want you to know the answers or be pushing your view of the diagnosis. I want to contact the person through the card, as an address." That seemed to be very recherché; a very obscure problem I was making. I don't think my teacher ever understood what the problem was, but it turned out that intuitive diagnosis is very easy to do. Although we don't understand its mechanism, any more than we understand the mechanism for remote viewing, I included an intuitive diagnosis session at the end of all my workshops. Doing an intuitive diagnosis of a person whose name is on a card is even easier than doing remote viewing of a location of a picture in an envelope. It's a more natural thing. People are really blown away when they get accurate [results]. I think that they incorporate the feeling tone of the sick person or the distant person. But that works anomalously well.

Mishlove: You've been doing workshops all over the world, now, and you've been doing it for decades. I am under the impression, from our conversations, that, typically speaking, when you do such a workshop, many if not most of the people in the workshop demonstrate successful remote viewing right off the bat.

Targ: That's right. I've done a lot of these things in Italy and in Esalen and other places. I had a thousand people in a so-called workshop in the desert recently. What I always tell the people [is], "You don't have to worry about anything. I will guarantee that everybody here will either have a psychic experience or see something psychic." The producers of the workshops are always very alarmed that all these people are going to want their money back. I've never had anybody ask for their money back. Not that everyone has a great psychic experience, but either the person themselves will have enough intuitive connection with my target or their nearest neighbor will have done something. So then everybody feels, even in a big group like that, like they've had contact with the target. I've gotten more confident about this over the years. Maybe, I've become more knowledgeable about what's available or more skillful about how to do it. I've gotten more courageous about what I'm willing to tell people is going to happen.

Mishlove: Russell, a thought just popped into my head. In fact, a phrase that I don't recall ever even thinking before. The phrase is a "psychic catalyst," a person around whom lots of psychic events occur, even if that person themselves is not highly engaged in psychic functioning. Now, I know you have been a successful remote viewer from time to time, but I think that possibly you, yourself, are functioning as a psychic catalyst so people in your presence seem to do better.

Targ: Well, there's a whole group of so-called psi-inductive experimenters. I was once in a workshop with William Braud, Marilyn Schlitz, and

Dean Radin, talking about psi-inducive experimenters. There was a time—this is maybe thirty years ago—where a sizable proportion of the published data belonged to just a handful of people. I think Dean Radin thought that fact was interesting. Maybe we should get those people together and see if they're doing something like one another.

For example, Marilyn was involved in an experiment at Duke University with Ramakrishna Rao. Rao had the idea that maybe a psychic could awaken anesthetized mice. The mice [were] anesthetized and then these little furry bundles would be divided, half would go to Marilyn and half would go to Rao. Time after time, Marilyn was much more successful in awakening the white mice It seemed obvious to me that the rats would rather wake up and see cheerful, energetic Marilyn than sleepy Ramakrishna Rao, an Indian meditator, more asleep than awake, one could say. The fact that the rats would wake up for Marilyn and not for Rao wasn't even surprising, on the face of it, but a prsi-conducive experimenter is even more conductive with rats.

Mishlove: Since you mentioned Marilyn Schlitz, I think it would be a service to let our viewers know about the study she did with the avowed skeptic Richard Wiseman in his laboratory, using a setup that he designed, where she served as the experimenter and got successful results. He tried to run the same experiment and the results were unsuccessful.

Targ: They were staring experiments. One group of people would be stared at by the experimenter and you measured their brain waves or skin resistance. Marilyn published several rounds of this experiment with William Braud, successfully. And she had done them successfully by herself. When she was invited to London University or Birkbeck College, she did them with Richard Wiseman. She was again successful, while Wiseman's group failed.

Mishlove: That's exactly what happened. As I recall, the staring was done from a distant location using video monitors. There was no possibility of any sensory leakage.

Targ: And that was a good, humbling experience for people who think we really know how the world works.

Mishlove: Let's talk about some of the unusual successes that are possible in remote viewing. I know even though Hella Hammid seemed to perform, statistically, ten times better than Pat Price, as I recall, Pat

Price was able to read code words from a secured NSA (National Security Agency) facility. A location once used as a target I gather, by the CIA in some of their experiments, much to the consternation of the NSA.

Mishlove: The Pat Price case is one that you focus on extensively in your documentary, *Third Eye Spies*. You certainly leave it as an open question as to whether there was some foul play or nefarious activity of some sort involved in his death. Since we're talking about the strength and reliability of remote viewing, it makes me wonder, and I've heard other people wonder, if a remote viewer gets too good, does that mean they will become a pawn in somebody else's game? Or that their life might be in danger?

Targ: If they're too good, and they're working for the CIA, they certainly could be in danger. While making the film, we had dozens of hours of film with Ken Kress, talking about Pat Price. It became clear that having an omniscient psychic working for them was very frightening. The CIA does their life's work in secrecy. And with Price around, there were no secrets. The problem with Price was that we eventually learned he was an enthusiastic Scientologist. He was sending each day's top-secret remote viewing narrative to his Scientology auditor, back at the Mother Church. We now know this because this information was released two years later, after the government broke into the Scientology [premises] looking for other things.

Now, if Price was handing this information over in the very beginning—Price was a smart man, but he was not a trained spy—so if he was meeting with the Scientologists or having regular phone calls with them or communicating in some other way by mail, it's very likely, in my opinion, [that] the CIA knew about it. He was doing top secret spying on foreign embassies for the CIA. Price was not security cleared. So that whole setup was very peculiar. The CIA had Farmer Price out in the pasture, coming into headquarters every day, then spying on the Libyan embassy; looking for their code room; looking for drug dealers, [and] doing all sorts of amazing things. All without a clearance. And he was handing in this information daily, to the Scientologists.

My uninformed guess is [that] the CIA must have known this after a few weeks of surveillance. It must have been obvious. They then had a problem. What do we do when Superman is a double agent? The psychic man who can see anything is also working for the Scientologists. That's a big problem. So, one question could be, would the Scientologists have killed Price because they were too nervous about what he was able to do psychically? Or the Russians may have killed him because he was a dangerous asset? Or he could have died because he had a heart attack? We don't know the answer. We have no privileged information. It's a mystery.

Mishlove: It seems to me that the thrust of our discussion, which is based—incidentally, I know, on a paper that you've written recently, submitted to a scientific journal—is that very highly reliable and strong results can be achieved with remote viewing. You seem to be suggesting that people can do that and work in a research context, or maybe even in the private sector, or in the military, without necessarily endangering themselves.

Targ: That's right. What we've shown is that psychic abilities are reliable and strong under the right conditions. It would be incorrect to say that ESP is weak and unreliable. In the end, I trained up six army officers who went back to Fort Meade, Maryland, who started a psychic army corps for the intelligence command; for INSCOM. That project went on for a decade. During that decade, they did 450 tasks for the CIA, DIA, and various other branches. For the DIA, they were called on to do 140 tasks. And they did thirty for the CIA. It proves they had satisfied customers. So, if your customer keeps coming back for 130 more, of what you gave them the first time, it seems like you're doing something reliable.

And, in fact, the INSCOM report on the first 750 trials done at Fort Meade, said 85% showed psychic ability, and half of those proved useful in an operational sense. That's all published. Well, I'm publishing it in my paper. This was published in proceedings that Ed May put out in four volumes. They revealed the final declassified records of the Stargate program, showing that innocent, untrained Stargate people, the people at Fort Meade, were practicing remote viewing. None of these people became famous psychics. These were people off the street. We showed them the moves and how to do remote viewing. In a decade, they had 450 tasks they were assigned by customers, who kept coming back again and again. Over hundreds of trials, requests came for more and more data, by the CIA and the Defense Intelligence Agency. So, I think the evidence is very strong that, whatever you think about psychic ability, Army Intelligence thought it was useful for over a decade.

Mishlove: Wouldn't it seem logical to you then, Russell, given this track record, which has been published, it's quite demonstrable, that remote viewing should be more widely and publicly applied today in the private sector, in the educational arena, and, of course, the government as well? It would seem to me that with that kind of a track record, the government would be foolish not to continue with remote viewing.

Targ: Well, I think it is very likely the government is continuing to do so. In fact, in the film, Kit Green says they probably still are doing remote viewing. Of the people that I trained, two of them were CIA agents who came to see what we were doing at SRI. They went back, and, in the 1970s, this same man and woman I trained were working with Pat Price. They had a little remote viewing coffee club at the CIA and were all doing tasks. It's now forty years past that. It would be surprising if you didn't have some remote viewing going on in the basement of the CIA today. That's what Kit Green says. I think that is probably true.

In society at large, in America, it's still not comfortable being a psychic. If psychic abilities are so powerful, why aren't there more? The answer would be that, in America, ESP is forbidden. Psychic ability is considered a sign of mental illness. In places like Iceland, or Brazil, or Holland, or even Soviet Siberia, psychic abilities are considered ordinary and desirable. For example, in Iceland, where I spent a bit of time, if a small child says, "I've been thinking about grandma. I think grandma's going to come and see us," In Iceland, the mother would set the table and say, "Grandma's probably coming for lunch. Maybe we should get ready for her appearance," then set the table. In New York, if your kid says, "I think grandma's coming," you reply, "Don't do that silly talk. Grandma is in California. She's not coming." Psychic abilities in Iceland are honored and considered important. In Brazil, they're considered a useful and everyday occurrence. I think there's certainly increasing interest in psychic ability. Our film is doing extremely well: *Third Eye Spies.* We're very happy about the results so far.

Mishlove: I'm glad to hear that, Russell. I'm very happy to continue to share your experience and your stories with our viewers, too. I think the bottom-line message seems to be that this stuff can work extremely well. There are still some, I suppose a researcher would call them, uncontrollable factors. There seems to be, I'll call it, the X factor. Some people for mysterious reasons, such as yourself, are highly successful, and other people who are just as enthusiastic are not. We have a lot yet to learn and the best way to learn is to continue to study the phenomena, as far as I'm concerned. Russell, thank you once again for being with me. I hope that we're able to have many more conversations like this to share with New Thinking Allowed viewers.

Targ: Thank you very much for talking with me, Jeffrey. I'm always happy to chat with you.

Mishlove: Likewise, Russell, you're one of my best friends.

13

Magic and Psi

Recorded on January 8, 2022

Jeffrey Mishlove: Our topic today is magic and psi. My guest is my good friend Russell Targ, the pioneer parapsychologist. Welcome, Russell. What a pleasure to be with you once again.

Russell Targ: Thank you, Jeffrey. I'm very happy to have a chance to chat with you.

Mishlove: We've known each other a very long time, for many decades. You have been engaged in parapsychology work for many, many years, but it's interesting to think that even before that, you were, as a teenager, an amateur magician.

That's what I tried to do in my work at Stanford Research Institute (SRI). I was always very openhearted, [with] very positive affect. We expect everything we do to be successful. This is not a test. This is a social agreement. I don't know where the people are hiding, but if you quiet your mind, we together can find out where the airplane has crashed, where the building is burning, where the Russians are testing a bomb, [or] where the aircraft carrier is moving. We can do all this crazy, amazing stuff. I don't know the answer, but I can help you because I know what psychic functioning sounds like. So, I'm the experimenter here. I'm a non-directive teacher. I'm just being kind to my visitor with the assumption that he's going to describe the right answer.

I did that for a decade at SRI and had anomalously good success. I will show you some of the things that I did, some of which are quite humorous. I did that for a decade. By and by people began to replicate it. There was a small group of Americans, like parapsychologists, who began to have very good results with non-directive experiments.

Chuck Honorton [1946-1992] was doing the Ganzfeld [experiment], and other people were doing that, too. In 1990, I organized a conference called "Increasing Psychic Reliability," with Russell Targ, William Broad [1942-2012], Rex Stanford [1938-2022], Marilyn Schlitz, and Chuck Honorton. We all decided conference criteria together. What we were concerned about is that 90% of the highly significant free response experiments were being done by 10% of the people. Most of the researchers were at this meeting. We wanted to know, why is it that Rex Stanford, Marilyn Schlitz, Russell Targ, and so forth, are getting four or five standard deviations, one in a million experiments, and other people are not seeing that.

We decided that the results you get in a free response trial are strongly dependent on how you interact with your subject. I, of course, have no training in that. I knew who Carl Rogers was, of course, but I had no training in how to do psychology experiments. I was a physicist. I entered ESP research with fifteen years' experience in laser physics, never having done a formal experiment in my life. What I had done is a lot of magic tricks.

Thinking about it this year, what I had been doing, my magic tricks in Chicago as a punky amateur magician—what did that have to do with my decade at SRI? I decided that doing magic is basically selling a situation, in the same way you sell a situation in remote viewing. I have a favorite card trick, which I'll briefly tell you. The illusion is, as they say, over the counter. The effect is, I shuffle a deck of cards, hand you the deck, you choose a card, and then I reveal my knowledge that I knew the card all along. Now, I did know the card all along, but the trick is, I wasn't shuffling the cards; you were not actually cutting the cards, [but] you have the strong experience.

I've done this for government scientists. Part of my credit for being able to do ESP research and get money from the government is that I was trained in magic. What does that mean? That means that I am less likely to be fooled by a visiting magician. For example, here's a deck of cards, regular cards; shuffle them up; choose one. Your card is the eight of clubs; that's the one my partner had written down an hour before in his notebook but that's impossible. How could he possibly have known the card? The answer is, my attention on you was to make you misapprehend what you clearly think you saw. That's what fake magic is. Misdirection is very powerful.

This little trick I described is called the magician's force, in which I am exposed to you saying, "That's not the card I chose; you can't make me do that." But in eighty years of doing the trick from a kid, I've never been caught. Nobody has ever caught me out saying, "That's bullshit, that's not the card I chose." Because the mechanics of this simple trick and the magic words you say are so powerful [that] the person is totally misdirected and unable to cognize what happens.

Of course, the fact that this goes on is very frightening, because you don't like to believe that in a face-to-face conversation, I can tell you it's blue, and you say it's green, even though it's not green. The reason I'm chatting with you now is, I believe, that my two decades of doing magic was good preparation for doing real magic at SRI. I would sit in the room there and tell a person, "I have no idea where your boss has gone to hide; he could be anywhere in the Bay Area, but you and I will be able to describe it. If you just close your eyes, tell me about the surprising images that appear in your awareness, and write those down. We will discover that the images that come into your awareness strongly correspond to where my partner Hal and your boss Joe have gone to hide, even though I have no idea where that could be."

It's as though I had created new magic words. I would never say, "We're going to try and find out where your boss has gone. Where do you think he's gone?" Even 1,200 years ago, the fellow on my wall, which I think is still visible, Padmasambhava, wrote a book called *Self-Liberation Through Seeing with Naked Awareness*. Naked awareness is quieting your mind, so you can experience what Dzogchen Buddhists call timeless awareness. You can move your consciousness freely into space, into time. Your consciousness is independent of time, so you're free of cause and effect. Importantly, he tells us 1,200 years ago, not to name nor grasp for what you want to see in the future; only allow it to come to you. Naming and grasping is the enemy of psychic functioning, and that was known 1,200 years ago—all written and ready for us to study.

My spiritual development was paid for by the Central Intelligence Agency (CIA). I sat in the dark for a decade, helping people quiet their mind and to describe where people were hiding. My preparation, as I said, was Dzogchen Buddhism and annoying amateur magic, which is, of course, not real magic. Now, I don't think that remote viewing is magical. Because I think that we now have some of the tools to understand how it's possible for a person to quiet his mind and describe what's going on in a distant place. Non-local functioning was first talked about by Albert Einstein in the 1930s, and Bell's Theorem came in 1965, and then [Stuart] Freedman and [John] Clauser at Berkeley demonstrated non-locality: that things can be separated and yet interact with each other across the distance. My colleague Hal Puthoff and I visited Freedman and Clauser in Berkeley, just as they had done this very important physics-changing experiment showing that things can be physically separated yet have a non-local connection.

So, non-locality has replaced magic. We live in a universe—this is my way of putting it, which would not be what all physicists would do—my view is that your consciousness transcends space and time. You can quiet your mind and see things as small as a proton in a hydrogen nucleus, as the Theosophical people did in the 1890s. They were able to describe the size of a proton. Ingo Swann can expand his awareness to describe what's happening on the surface of Jupiter, 500 million miles away. Distance doesn't matter, down to 10^{-10} microns and as far out as Jupiter. So, our consciousness is free to move through space and time, and that's what our experiments show.

Mishlove: Russell, I'd like to go back to remarks you made in earlier interviews about Robert Rosenthal and the Pygmalion effect. Most people assume that it really has nothing to do with non-locality or with the paranormal; that if the teacher is nicer to these students because the teacher has high expectations, the students will then perform better. But I gather from our conversation that you seem to be suggesting there's a non-local or a paranormal component to the Pygmalion effect.

Targ: No, Jeffrey, I think that there are two phenomena going on now. If somebody comes into my lab and we're going to do an experiment, if they think this is a test, that makes it infinitely harder than if they feel like we are going on a little trip. The Pygmalion effect is not a metaphysical phenomenon. It's a manifestation of being kind to your students. If you're kind to your students, you can help the student manifest an ability that he has that he didn't know he had. So, people come into my lab and some would say, "I don't believe in this stuff. This is all BS. I'm here to find out how you're doing this." And I said, "This is not a test. We'll just do this together. Don't worry about it."

My annoying words are, "If you just do what I tell you to do, this will all come out fine. You don't have to worry about anything."

Now, that's not paranormal. What I'm doing that's paranormal is helping the person move his awareness into the distance or into the future. That's a paranormal non-local phenomenon. But the key to doing that is to make the person feel comfortable and to make them feel that what I'm asking them to do is not crazy, which is what they think it is. Rosenthal's idea is that the way you treat your subject has a big effect on how they behave. That can be an IQ test, which is not a metaphysical phenomenon, or it can be finding a downed airplane in Russia, which is a non-local phenomenon. Did I answer your question?

Mishlove: Well, yes and no, because I have known you for a long time and I think it may be hard to acknowledge, but I'm under the impression that there's something about your very presence that exudes—I mean, you could call it magic. For example, when you were doing magic tricks as a child, as I recall from one of our conversations, you won a couple of prizes that were kind of unexpected. I wonder if it has anything to do with real magic. Many magicians are interested in the metaphysical side of magic.

What this experience suggests to me, Russ, is that in addition to the fact that you were very nice to your research subjects, there's something about you and your native psi ability that kind of rubs off on people who work with you in the enclosed chamber, the sealed room where you did your remote viewing experiments at SRI.

Targ: My little spider web. I'm not shy about claiming that I may have some psychic ability, but there are dozens of other people doing remote viewing: army officers in their army boots out of Fort Meade; I trained six people how to do remote viewing, and they set up a whole army psychic corps at Fort Meade. That was the formal Star Gate program. I trained the first six people, but I was at least two people removed from a lot of work that went on there. I think that I do well, what I'm doing in the shielded room, but it's not unique to Russ Targ. I'm happy to talk to you. We have a puzzle, and I'm happy to share that with you. I'm not alone as a psychic.

Shortly after the program got started, we published a paper in 1974 in *Nature* magazine about our early experiments with Pat Price. We described all sorts of distant things that were hidden around the Bay Area. My editor was also the editor of Richard Bach, the *Jonathan Livingston Seagull* author. She said, "Richard Bach is interested in your work. He's a very mystical pilot. He'd like to meet you. Besides, he just made ten million dollars from this book that I published for him." Richard flew the airplane into Palo Alto, came to the lab and said, "I'd like to see something psychic." That's what people always say. They want me to demonstrate some psychic thing to them. My answer always is, "I'm not going to do that, because you'll then think it's a trick. But I will show you how to do it, and then you can go away with the drawing that you made. We'll send Hal, my partner, to hide someplace, and I have no idea where he's going; no idea at all. And you and I will find him."

So, Hal went someplace. Richard said, "I see Hal is in a building, a very tall building with tall cutouts inside, a very decorative building. He's now walking to the end of the building. There is like a counter; it looks like an airplane ticket counter. He's standing at this long, shiny counter, three feet wide and eight feet long," says Richard. "On the wall behind the counter is the logo of the company. That's what I get."

Okay, so Hal came back, and I said, "Well, where were you? It sounded like a very peculiar place." He said, "Well, I went to the big church on Hamilton Avenue, a tall pointy building. At the end of the church, there's this long altar," and behind the altar on the wall is, of course, the logo of the company, which is a big cross.

Methodist sanctuary, Palo Alto, CA.

So, Richard thought this was very amusing. He liked this. He took a picture. His picture greatly resembled what he had seen. I had no idea where he [Hal] had gone. But this is the kind of thing that a person will do. [They] come into the lab, "I don't know anything about remote viewing. What am I supposed to do?" I just sit and say, "Hal has gone someplace. Tell me what you see."

Mishlove: You have had a remarkable track record taking people with no experience, like Hella, for example, and the very first time they endeavor to do remote viewing, they get a direct hit. Ultimately what I did in that session once you straightened me out a little bit. On the other hand, your partner Hal Puthoff worked very hard with Ingo Swann to develop a very elaborate training method. There's been this sort of conflict in the field ever since then, it seems to me, as to what is the role of training? If people can get perfect hits the first time, do they really need training, or do they just need to have a session with Russell Targ?

Targ: I don't think the training is successful. People have copied coordinate remote viewing and different kinds of remote viewing protocols as training. My opinion is, once you show them the moves, once you give them the experience, they go off and do it. Like learning to ride a unicycle, it looks like it's quite impossible. But once you put a person with good balance, like my daughter, as a five-year-old, I remember, put her on the unicycle, balance her up, and off she rode. She rode her unicycle in nursery school every day for a semester. As a three-year-old, I (sic) would take her to the children's park in Rinconada Park, where you could play in the sand or play on the seesaw. She amused herself by walking on the top ridge of the wire fence around the park. She just had naturally excellent balance and had no problem hopping on a unicycle and riding away. She did not need any further lessons.

We had finished our trials with Pat Price. We'd done nine trials of the form: You and I are sitting in the laboratory. Hal is hiding someplace, as though he's been kidnapped. What do you see? What comes to view? Pat described nine different places on those nine trials. Seven of those were judged first place, which would be odds of one in 100,000. Or to put it simply, if Hal had been kidnapped nine times by the terrorists, Price would have named the place seven out of the nine times. Price would have named where he was hidden seven out of the nine times. The CIA thought this was very important and renewed our program. They weren't interested in the one in 100,000. They were interested in the fact that Pat could say they've gone to a church, they've gone to the windmill, they've gone to the waterfall, and that was where he had been nine times in a row. And we published that in *Nature*.

With Hella—we had now worked with Ingo Swann, who's a natural psychic. We worked with Pat Price, who's a natural psychic. Kit Green, who's head of the Life Science Division at CIA, said, "I want to see somebody who's not a natural psychic. Can't you find an ordinary person?" So, I asked Hella Hammid, who would in no sense be called ordinary. She was a highly intelligent, cultivated German photographer, and a good friend of our family. She thought it would be very amusing to be paid by the CIA to be psychic, which is not something she ever had any thoughts about. So, she said, "Sure, I'll come to Palo Alto and pretend to be a psychic. If you show me what to do, I'll do that. I'm very good at following instructions."

For the first trial we sat in my little shielded room. She had crocheted little stockings for herself where each toe had an eyeball. She had these eyeball socks to give all the importance we could for the CIA project. I said, "Hal has gone to hide somewhere. Nobody knows where it is. Can you tell me about the images that come to your awareness?" She said, "I see something moving fast up high. I know that a judge will never be able to match that." So, I say, "Let's take a break and take a deep breath. Let's look again. We're looking for Hal. He's someplace in the Bay Area. Don't know where he is. What do you see?" She said, "It's like a trough up in the air. It couldn't hold any water because it's full of holes, but there's a trough up in the air." I said, "That's very interesting. Let's take a break and maybe you can draw that." She said, "Okay." She made this drawing of squares within squares within squares, which is now an iconic image of the pedestrian overpass.

Very accurate drawing of the overpass, as you would see from where she is standing. That was, of course, the number one match and her number one trial. And as you mentioned, this is Hella's very first effort at remote viewing. So, once again, I don't know the answer, but I know what the answer is going to sound like.

Mishlove: Interesting that it was the very same highway overpass that was the target in my first trial.

Targ: We have a target pool of 60 targets. To the best of my knowledge, it's the only time the same target came up twice. Now, for statistical reasons, we want to do this with replacement, as you understand, because if you get a church—for example, we got a church with Richard

Bach—we don't want to diminish the number of churches. If whoever put it together tried to have a certain number of overpasses, or a certain number of churches, you don't want to diminish that statistical occurrence by pulling them out.

Now, one of my favorite stories to tell, which I have never told to anybody publicly, but our lab manager was concerned about what's going on. All that I'm describing is, in a certain sense, what's happening behind the curtain. All this remote viewing is me in the dark with the viewer. SRI has no idea what I am doing in the dark with the viewer.

So, they brought in a very famous Israeli physicist, Yakir Aharonov, a person I knew well from his technical work with David Bohm, the famous Aharonov-Bohm Effect. I don't even have to tell you what it's about. So, he's a famous Nobel candidate. Didn't get a Nobel Prize, but if he lives long enough, he may get one. I'd never met him before, of course. He was brought to our lab because SRI wanted to know, am I working with softhearted psychics? Aharonov was not such a person.

He and I sat down. We could talk about physics. I said, "Hal and your friend have gone to hide someplace. I have no idea where they are." He said, "It doesn't matter to me. I don't even believe in this stuff. Doesn't make any sense. Certainly not physics. What do you want me to do?" I said, "Hal and your buddy are probably at an interesting place now in the San Francisco Bay Area. Can you tell me what comes to view when you close your eyes?" He said, "I don't know about you. When I close my eyes, it's dark." We did that for almost 20 minutes. I said, "They're just about done now. Can you tell me, do any images come to view?" He said, "No, I told you. It's dark when I close my eyes." I said, "I understand that. Let's pretend that you see something"—my best Rogerian technique. I said, "Pretend you see something. Can you tell me what comes to mind if you just make something up?" He said, "Well, what comes to mind is my mother's farm in Israel, where she raises ducks. I see a duck crossing the road." I said, "That's wonderful. Could you draw that for me, please?" He made a very cute little drawing of a duck crossing the road. Your ESP will tell you that the place they had gone to in Palo Alto was the duck pond by the Palo Alto airport. So, the target on the piece of paper, that they went with, had driving instructions that go to the duck pond, and the arch psychic from Israel drew him a picture of a duck.

Mishlove: Do you think that changed his attitude at that point?

Targ: I don't think it changed Aharonov's attitude, but it changed the attitude of our lab manager, because this is like a 100% match from a very trustworthy person of his choosing. So, they were quite convinced. I had one other person like that worth talking about. We were now lined up to get a million dollars a year working with the US Army. We had a visit from Walter LaBerge [1924-2004], who was Undersecretary of Defense. We had this secret program at SRI. Nobody knows it's the Army. LaBerge comes flying in on a helicopter. We must clear our parking lot so this guy can come flying in his helicopter. Everybody wants to know what Puthoff and Targ are doing, that you've got the Undersecretary of Defense; what kind of program is this?

LaBerge and his Major come upstairs, and I get to meet them, and they get to meet Hal. Then they go hide someplace, the Major and Hal. Again, the story you've become accustomed to, LaBerge says, "I don't believe in this. Can't you have Ingo Swann or somebody do this? I didn't plan to be a psychic here. I planned to watch a demo." I said, "If I do a demo, I could do that. I could have Ingo Swann tell you where Hal and the Major have gone. But then you'd go back to Washington, and you and your Major would try and figure out how the trick was done. How did I deceive you? How did I get you to believe this was the answer? But on the other hand, if you just close your eyes and draw a picture of where they are, then you'll have your own picture and your own experience to guide you. You'll have that back in Washington."

And he did that. He drew that they had gone to a place called Allied Arts, north of SRI. He said, "I see a lot of bricks, a circular brick structure with a fountain in the middle." That's exactly where they were. If you ever look up Allied Arts, he drew a wonderful little sketch of the bricks in the fountain. And we got the contract. Basically, with these various people, we had to earn our way. If you claim you're doing something psychic, show me what you're doing.

So even with skeptical people like Aharonov and LaBerge, who don't believe in it, don't want to do it, I sort of soften it so they don't have to do anything that's weird. I don't say, "Where are they hiding?" which is an obviously impossible task. I just cue it up and explain to them, "You can't do this wrong. All I want to know is what you're experiencing. I just want you to tell me about the surprising images that come into your awareness. And only you know that. So, if you will share that with me, then we'll be able to find the people that are hiding." If you think of this as a magic trick, those are the magic words. "Just close your eyes and tell me about the surprising images that come into your awareness." Then they will do that exact thing and we'll be able to find them.

180

Mishlove: Russell, you've been one of the most successful parapsychology researchers in history. You have been doing this work now for half a century. I know you worked with groups of people all over the world, teaching them to do the very same thing. I wonder if you have any thoughts about where all of this interest in remote viewing—and now there are, I think, tens of thousands of people practicing remote viewing—what is it all leading to?

Targ: It leads people to the idea that there's more to the nature of their body and soul than meat and potatoes. They can quiet their mind and experience the universe. The Buddhists teach us to expand our awareness outside of space and time, and get rid of the suffering that comes from thinking that you don't have enough or that you're in danger. You can move to a much freer spirit. It gives you freedom. It gives you freedom to move your awareness from craving to a limitless dimension. I wrote a book called *Limitless Mind* that answers your question.

I can do this in a workshop with a hundred people. They will describe my little object and that experience is mind-changing to them. It's like I've given them a new sense, a new eyeball. Learning to do remote viewing doesn't give you a new belief system. It just gives you a new capability. One other thing, if you're of a spiritual inclination, it gives you something to do in a meditation. In meditation, you can move into this timeless awareness that's available. Remote viewing is not a spiritual path, incidentally. It's a capability, like vision or hearing, but it can lead you onto a spiritual path because it allows you to quiet your mind and expand your awareness. So, the reward for learning remote viewing is not that you can win the lottery—although you may be able to do that anyway—it's to control your mind so that it basically gives you access to the off switch. I don't know if that answers your question.

Mishlove: Actually, I'm thinking about how it began with funding from NASA, funding from the CIA, funding from the Army, and yet it's pointing in the direction of something having to do with human potential and metaphysics and I think also, spirituality.

Targ: It certainly pertains to spirituality, but it doesn't have anything to do with deities. It gives you contact with your spiritual nature. What the physicist would say is that your non-spiritual nature says that you are meat and potatoes. If you think that's the answer, if you think that is who you are and what you see in the mirror each morning, you're in for a lot of suffering. What you see in the mirror in the morning, in general, does not get increasingly beautiful over time. It goes the other direction. So, if you think that's who you are, it's a lot of suffering. But, if you think that who you are is of timeless awareness, the mental capability to expand your awareness and move out into time and space—that gives you a huge capability for meditation—for going to sleep. Jung had an experience like that; Carl Jung. He describes this in his *Memories, Dreams, Reflections* book. He had an out-of-body experience where he went out past the moon. Then he looks back at the earth and the stars and the moon, and that changes his whole view of human capabilities.

Mishlove: Russell, before we end the interview and looking back on your long career, as you say, you've been practicing magic for 80 years. I know that your 88th birthday is coming up this year. Do you have any other thoughts you'd like to share with our viewers?

Targ: Like what have I been doing for the past 88 years? Well, I spent half of that time as a physicist building lasers, flying lasers through thunderstorms and giant lasers for cutting up locomotive cylinders. The other half I spent in the spiritual realm, studying psychic abilities. So, if I were to give anyone advice, I would certainly suggest that you become accustomed to remote viewing capabilities. If you can control the chatter of your mind and open your mind to see into the distance, see into the future—When you're going to sleep, for example, you can't go to sleep, something you can do with your chattering mind is move off the planet into the distance, into the future, where there are no distractions.

Mishlove: Russell, this has been a delightful conversation. Is there anything else on your agenda that you'd like to share?

Targ: I think you've been very generous in giving me an opportunity to tell people what I've been doing. We're celebrating the 50th anniversary of remote viewing at SRI. Indeed, I'll have an 88th birthday in April. In June, we're celebrating the 50th anniversary of Bobby Fischer becoming the world chess champion. Fischer was my brother-in-law. He was a brother of my former wife, Joan Fischer. So, we're going to have a lot of things to celebrate.

Mishlove: I look forward, Russell, to more years with you. I know you and I both have gone through different health issues. I think we both have pacemakers at this point. So, I know we're getting older, but it's always a great joy for me to have time with you like this and to be able to share it with the *New Thinking Allowed* audience.

Targ: Thank you very much for the opportunity. And again, congratulations on your great accomplishment, winning the Grand Prize in the Bigelow Institute essay competition. I'm very, very happy for you, Jeffrey. It does my heart good that you won this wonderful prize.

Mishlove: I feel like you had a big part in it. You were part of the essay and, as I shared with you, a big part of the acceptance speech as well.

Targ: Thank you. I was very happy to be there.

14

Remote Viewing From the Inside Out

Recorded on February 14, 2022

Jeffrey Mishlove: Today we'll be looking at remote viewing from the inside out. Back by popular demand is my good friend Russell Targ who will be celebrating his 88th birthday this year. Russell was the co-founder of the remote viewing program at Stanford Research Institute (SRI) International in Menlo Park, California. With his partner Harold (Hal) Puthoff he co-authored the book, *Mind Reach: Scientists Look at Psychic Abilities*. It was a landmark book that put remote viewing on the map. Subsequently, Russell has written many other books. Welcome, Russell. It's a pleasure once again to be with you today.

Russell Targ: I'm happy to be able to wish you a happy Valentine's Day. I appreciate the opportunity to talk about my favorite subject, finish up the work we did at Stanford Research Institute and move on to something beyond that.

Mishlove: As I recall, in our last conversation we spent a lot of time talking about your knowledge of remote viewing and your experiences with what is traditionally called "the monitor" in remote viewing experiments. But you have also had experience as a percipient or a subject, as a remote viewer yourself. I know it goes back probably even to your childhood. But I'm very interested to begin to talk about an experience you had when you were at SRI working with Pat Price [1918-1975] and he couldn't show up so you suddenly, without any warning, were asked to stand in for him as the subject in a remote viewing trial.

Targ: That's right, Jeffrey. The incident you're talking about is that we had done several successful remote viewings with Pat Price. In the last one we did, Price described a weapons factory in Soviet Siberia, which was highly successful. He had talked about a big crane and spheres underground and everyone was very excited.

That was a turning point in the program. The Central Intelligence Agency (CIA) had invited, or coerced, Price to leave the program and go [to] live in Virginia. Hal was going on his vacation for the first time to take a break from the program and I was doing a last remote viewing series with the great psychic Pat Price. What I was involved with is sitting with Price in our little shielded room and, each day for five days, he was going to describe where Hal Puthoff was somewhere in South America. Typical remote viewing.

Here we are, Russell Targ and Pat Price. "Pat, what do you see?" One day he would say, "I see a volcano." Another day he would see a harbor. Another day he would see a market. On day four he might see a church. And on day five, he didn't show up. I'm sitting in my little wire cage, Russell Targ and Pat Price doing remote viewing, and I plaintively said in the tape recorder, "It looks like Pat's not gonna show up, so I'll have to do it myself." I knew this was a serious group of experiments. We really wanted to know whether Pat or somebody else would be able to describe what Hal was doing and where he was two thousand miles away in Colombia, South America.

Mishlove: Had you ever, at this point, participated in a formal remote viewing trial?

Targ: I had not. They specifically didn't want the researchers to be involved in the experiments because it looks bad. We don't want to mix the psychics with the scientists. But this was a case where there was nobody else to do it and I knew that we wanted to continue the series. I just said, "This is remote viewing with Russell Targ and Pat Price." It's some date or other in 1974, probably June of 1974, because we knew that Price was going to leave shortly. I said, "Price is not here so I will do it myself. I'll close my eyes and describe what I see." I'm sitting in this little wire cage and close my eyes and what I'm looking at appeared to be an island airport. That was the gestalt. I said, "On the right side is some grass and sand and on the left side it looks like an airport building. It looks like at the end of the airport there is the ocean." I'm looking at this airport with ocean at the end of the runway, sand and grass on the right, airport building on the left, a complete scene. I thought, "I'll draw that."

It came to pass that Hal returned from Columbia and he, on that day, had been given an invitation to fly out to an island airport called San Andreas Island. I now have pictures of the island. I have a picture of the airport and it turned out that the drawing that I made was really a first-class remote viewing. The payoff, the reason we're still talking about it, is that it shows that remote viewing is so easy that even a scientist can do it.

Mishlove: As you describe the way it all came down to you, it sounds as if you're already interpreting what you saw right away. It's an airport rather than just the raw sensory impressions.

Targ: That's right. I didn't behave in the way a remote viewer is supposed to. I would say to a viewer, "What are you experiencing that makes you think it's an airport?" In this case, I would say, because it looks exactly like an airport. I see a runway. I see an airport building on the left and the runway runs into the ocean. That's what I see so that's what I'm going to draw. It turned out that my drawing greatly corresponded to what was there. Our management didn't like the fact that I was participating in an experiment because the psychics and the scientists were not supposed to mix. On the other hand, people recognized that it was an outstanding drawing, so I am happy that I overstepped the bounds in this instance.

Mishlove: In effect, what you did is broke two of the so-called standard rules of separating the scientists from the psychics, and of coming up right off the bat with an interpretation of your impressions, which suggests to me that breaking the rules is sometimes the right thing to do.

Targ: That's right. In experiments we did with Joe McMoneagle, his very first remote viewing when we chose him from one of six Army recruits, he covered a page with little drawings, one of which was a quite good-looking architectural drawing of the Stanford Art Museum: a three-dimensional drawing. I said, "You've got a lot of drawings here on the page, could you choose one and make it clearer so that a poor judge won't have to look at nine or ten drawings? Help the judge. Which one of these do you like?" Of course, he liked the art museum and made a splendid three-dimensional drawing of that. The judges had no trouble choosing that. And we had no trouble choosing Joe to be part of the Army program.

Mishlove: Joe McMoneagle himself has often said, don't be afraid of what is sometimes disparagingly called analytical overlay. Sometimes what you think is an analytical overlay is an accurate depiction of the target.

Targ: That's right. That requires experience to separate what Ingo Swann calls separating the psychic signal from the mental noise. You must watch out for memory and imagination. If you're doing remote viewing and the first thing that comes to mind is an orange Volkswagen, we would say, debrief that, put down an orange Volkswagen at the top of the page. Call it an analytical overlay, and let's see what else shows up. We would never say, cross that out, don't pay attention to that. But if something that analytical shows up, we would honor the experience, set it aside, and go on and see what else is there.

Mishlove: In your case, in this trial, your very first formal remote viewing trial, did you prep in any way for it? You just closed your eyes and reported the mental imagery? What else might you have done?

Targ: I'm pretty good at just closing my eyes and visualizing the thing that I'm looking for, which will come up whole as an image, clearly. I haven't done that for the SRI program, but I certainly have done it in my life. People have the idea that I can find things. It's not uncommon for somebody, especially in the family. My daughter had written a term paper, and she couldn't find it. I was able to visualize that and tell her she'd put it in her dresser drawer. Or, my daughter would want me to find her notebook or something like that.

Mishlove: Before you did your very first formal trial at SRI, had you ever engaged as a percipient of remote viewing informally?

Targ: In fact, I had an experience with our friend, Charlie Tart, the parapsychologist. We were together sitting around the fireplace. I was sitting cross-legged and meditating, as he was, and I had this kundalini experience. I could feel the energy; it's a nice feeling. The reason that people do kundalini is not to blow their brains out but to have the feeling of the energy from the kundalini meditation. It was maybe stimulated by the fireplace, but I felt like a fire was going up my back, up my spine. I was aware that people say this is a dangerous thing to do without a teacher, as many things in life are. I just stood up and sort of

188

waved my arms and terminated that experience, but I was far enough into kundalini, so I understood the process and the hazards. I knew about Gopi Krishna, for example, who became a well-known Hindu meditator and expert in kundalini after having a very bad experience that hospitalized him. He wrote a book about the dangers of kundalini without a teacher.

Mishlove: I presume you stopped the kundalini practice after that.

Targ: That's right. I'm still a meditator but I am not doing the kundalini, especially now that I'm an old man. I don't have any brain cells to spare. I think that kundalini is way too dangerous for me. I'm just an ordinary hatha yoga, shamatha [tranquility of mind] yoga meditator.

Mishlove: I used to practice kundalini yoga as part of the 3HO program initiated by Yogi Bhajan.

Targ: So you already know this big book that I have.

Mishlove: Arthur Avalon is sort of from a different lineage but yes, of course, that's a wonderful book.

Targ: *The Serpent Power*, 500 pages of instruction on how to blow out your brain.

Mishlove: Let me ask you this. How does the kundalini meditation, as you recall it, differ from just regular meditation?

Targ: Kundalini meditation is quite—in regular meditation you're trying to be quiet and empty your visual field. In kundalini you have in mind to raise the serpent power. This is the meditation where you are actually doing something. In normal hatha yoga or shamatha [tranquility of mind] meditation you're trying to be quiet.

Mishlove: The kundalini meditation of Yogi Bhajan focused on a technique he called the breath of fire, which is very short and rapid breaths, that involved the diaphragm quite a bit. I'm assuming that you were practicing something other than that.

Targ: That's right. I was trying to do it—Avalon's book was written in the early 1900s and reprinted numerous times. I was trying to operate from his [book].

Mishlove: The interesting thing to me here, Russell, is that prior to you ever engaging in formal research as a parapsychologist you had had this spontaneous—I'll call it a spontaneous remote viewing or clairvoyant experience. You had been engaged with the Theosophical Society. You were practicing kundalini meditation and other forms of meditation. I think that all those things are great preparation for somebody going into parapsychology, in spite of the notion that somehow the scientists must be objective and not participate subjectively in these sorts of activities.

Targ: I would say that that's true. In parapsychology, researchers can go into psychokinesis, which is enthusiastically followed by people. But the effect size for psychokinesis is about one percent of the effect size for visualizing things, telepathy, and clairvoyance. So if I was going to bet my career on something, it was not going to be psychokinesis but rather it would be perceptual effects.

Mishlove: You use the term predestination. I wonder what you think about that. I know you've done a lot of work in the whole area of precognition. I don't think you doubt that precognition is successful, but it certainly does imply that the future already exists somewhere.

Targ: That's right. Pauli was interested in acausality and synchronicity because he had precognitive dreams. I've had some very striking precognitive dreams. In fact, my precognitive dreams are probably the most striking psychic occurrences in my life.

Mishlove: If the future already exists, as these experiences suggest, that would imply to many people that we don't really have free will. You sort of intimated this when you said you didn't know how it is that you seemed to be so successful at SRI. Maybe our sense of free will is an illusion. Do you have a sense of that yourself, Russell?

Targ: I think you have free will, but not as much as you think. I believe in physics, and I believe in causality. I think that the little wagon that you push begins to move after you push it, not before you push it. I believe Newton's law of F=ma is correct, that events have causes; however, we don't always know what those causes are. I think that by and large we live in a causal world. The physicists can't give up causality. But even as Pauli said, causality is statistical. That's quite a breakthrough for Wolfgang Pauli to begin to talk about statistical causality because his whole life was about causality. But he had precognitive dreams, and he knew that he could screw up experiments from a distance. He was aware that causality, although it exists, is not hard and fast. I agree with that.

Mishlove: To jump around a little bit, another topic that I find of interest is a study that you engaged in. I was involved in it peripherally. I think back in the 1990s you were working with our mutual friend Dean Brown and his wife Wendy. At that time your remote viewing partner was Jane Katra. The study ended up being published in the *Journal of Scientific Exploration.* You were a remote viewing percipient for several trials in that study.

Targ: That is true. You've unmasked me. Jane and I were the viewers. Dean and Wendy, who are mathematicians, were the judges. This was a somewhat complicated experiment because it was redundancy coding. That is, Wendy would choose two targets for Jane. Dean would choose two targets for me, and these corresponded to silver going up or down. I not only had to describe the target that Dean had, but I had to describe the one that corresponded to silver going in the direction it was going, and we couldn't know that. Our hypothesis was that if I described the crystal cake dish, which meant silver is going up, and Jane described the coffee grinder, which meant that silver is going up, we could bet on silver going up. What you needed to bet in the market, theoretically, is excellent viewings of something and we had to agree that the something would both be in the same direction, either up or down. It was redundancy coding.

We did a dozen of those trials each. You were allowed to pass. If you didn't think it was any good you could pass. If I would describe something and Dean would say, that doesn't correspond to either of my targets, we would pass. Of the things that were judged we had eleven out of twelve that were correct. That's highly significant odds, of almost one in a thousand. Of the things that were made paper trades, six out of seven of our viewings were correct for the direction of silver moving. That shows that even inexperienced people with a good protocol and a good supportive environment can do this kind of thing.

As you know, years earlier I had done a similar experiment with Keith Harary, who was an experienced psychic. We made nine forecasts for silver in the real market and all nine of our forecasts were correct. We made $120,000 and were displayed on the front page of the *Wall Street Journal.*

That got a lot of attention. We were not successful the following year, which disappointed a lot of people, but we have explanations for that. The simple explanation is that our investor wanted to do two trials a week because we were making so much money. If you do two trials a week it means that the viewer does not get feedback for the first trial until after he's done the second trial. That's very bad because he needs feedback to be successful. We published that in the *Journal of Scientific Exploration.*

Mishlove: Would you say, Russell, that your experience in that experiment done in the 1990s was any different than the experience you had in 1974 at SRI, the day that Pat Price didn't show up?

Targ: No. I would say it was very similar. Dean would say, "I've got something interesting for you. Tell me about the object I'm going to show you later." I would just close my eyes. In some of those instances I gave very sharp, correct descriptions. I still remember this cut glass cake dish that was circular on the bottom and rectangular and square on the top; [a] very unusual, large cake dish of an unusual shape that I described correctly. Another thing he had was a child's rattle, which was shaped like a bone with a bell on each end. I described this plastic thing. I may have even said with something shaky on each end. A number of those times I had very sharp descriptions.

Mishlove: You used basically the same simple method: just close your eyes and report the imagery that comes up.

Targ: You are looking for a surprising image. The shibboleth that I created is: you close your eyes and look for something surprising that comes to your attention. That seems to be very helpful. You do not have to eat porridge at the feet of your guru. You do not have to pay a teacher thousands of dollars. Remote viewing is very easy to do. I'm writing a new book that I told you about, *Mind Beyond Space and Time: Learning Remote Viewing from the Masters.* I'm not the master. We have Hella Hammid, Ingo Swann, Pat Price, [and] Joe McMoneagle, all describing what their process is. I'm halfway through this book. I hope to publish it this year sometime.

Mishlove: It's wonderful that you're still active and talking about remote viewing, Russell, after all these years. I know you have many more stories to tell. We haven't gotten to them all. I hope we can schedule yet another interview in the future. But, for the time being, I want to thank you once again so much for being with me and with the *New Thinking Allowed* audience.

Targ: Thank you very much for the opportunity. It's always a great pleasure to be here with you and talk about my favorite subject. Thank you very much, Jeffrey.

15

Precognitive Dreaming

Recorded on May 14, 2023

Jeffrey Mishlove: Today we'll be looking at precognitive dreaming. My guest is my good friend Russell Targ. Russell is one of the founders of the discipline of Remote Viewing. Russell recently turned 89 years old. He lives in Palo Alto, California. Welcome, Russell. What a pleasure to be with you again.

Russell Targ: I'm very happy to be with you to talk about my favorite subject: looking into the distance and looking into the future.

Mishlove: I know you've been doing a lot of work with your dreams, Russell. Maybe for starters you could share with our viewers what your approach is in terms of capturing precognitive events in your dreams.

Targ: Capturing precognitive dreams is a lot like remote viewing. You ask people to try and clear their minds before they go into the session. With precognitive dreams, my experience is that most people have had precognitive dreams. In fact, most people's first contact with psychic abilities is a precognitive dream. But, if you're going to use a precognitive dream, you have to be able to get rid of your anxiety dreams, your wish fulfillment dreams, [and] your dreams cluttered up from the previous day's residue. Look for dreams of unique characterization: very crisp, very unusual, [and] bizarre. If you're having a dream that's very startling—basically, if you dream about failing a math test and you haven't studied for the math test, we will not consider that precognitive. You're looking for a dream, which is totally free of your previous day's residue and unusually clear and bizarre in its character.

For the past half year, I've been following that protocol with my wife Patricia. I do not write down my dreams, sorry to say, but I have a lot of dreams. I've been eager to separate the true precognitive dreams from the annoying regular dreams. My plan is that I get credit in the "big book" for a precognitive dream if I tell my wife about the dream before it occurs. So, if I have a precognitive dream or a dream I think is precognitive, I'll wake up and say, "Is it based on the check that I wrote yesterday or the dinner that I had last night, or, is this really free of my usual bellyaches and has nothing to do with my ordinary life and is crystal clear?"

With this protocol I make a certain number of Type I errors, that is, I have dreams, which turn out to be precognitive. I don't tell Patty about them because they don't meet my protocol, as I said it. A Type II error would be telling her about a dream which doesn't come to pass, and that would be very bad. This is like remote viewing. We can skip a couple of pretty good remote viewings that aren't right, but we're very averse to any kind of errors. So, [in] the past half year I have not told Patty about any dream which failed to come true. We want to avoid announcing precognitive dreams, which are not really going to come true.

This is like when I was at Lockheed [Martin]. We were looking for a wind shear using lasers. It was very important never to fail to announce the wind shear that a plane is going to run into and consequently crash, as a Type I error. You don't want any of those. It's not good if you announce the wind shear and it doesn't occur. That's bad for your publicity, yet nobody gets killed. In my work with Patricia, I'm willing to miss an occasional hot dream that comes true. I'm very eager not to damage my credibility with my wife by saying, "I had this fabulous dream; let me tell you about it," and nothing happens. In the past half year, I have never told her about a dream that failed to occur.

Mishlove: How good are you at remembering your dreams, since you don't write them down?

Targ: I'm excellent at remembering dreams with detail. When I wake up from a dream, I can tell you on and on and on about what happened, who was there, [and] what they wore.

Mishlove: Were you always good at remembering your dreams like this?

Targ: Yeah, I've always been good at remembering dreams. It's only, I would say, [in] the past half-year that I've had very sharp precognitive dreams. Some dreams, which we may get to at the end, are very complicated dreams. You must wait fifteen minutes before you realize that you're sort of caught up in a spider's web of weird dreams, manifesting one bit at a time, but we're not going to do that tonight.

The thing that I want to emphasize is that from our work at SRI and the work at Princeton College, most psychical researchers are now convinced that precognition is as strong and reliable a phenomenon as remote viewing into the distance. Occasionally, working with army volunteers totally unfamiliar with remote viewing or psychics or any of that stuff, we were picking out the people who were going to take part in the army ESP program at Fort Meade. This became the Stargate program. Some of these people had not a clue what I was asking them to do. They'd say, "I have no idea where they're hiding." I'd say, "I know that, but why don't we just do it this way. Your boss has gone to hide somewhere with Hal. I have no idea where it could be at all, but we will all meet there in a half hour, you and me and Hal and your boss. We will all meet there. I just want you to quiet your mind and tell me about the surprising images that appear in your awareness pertaining to where we're going to be in a half hour. We don't know where it is but we will be someplace. Tell me what is the surprising image that shows up." I would say that works a hundred percent of the time, in my experience.

Mishlove: You seem particularly gifted as a catalyst for psychic functioning. I know as a researcher you have a track record that's almost unparalleled in the field of parapsychology. As we've discussed in several of our previous interviews, I think there's something about you, Russell, and your charisma that's a factor. Some of our viewers will probably wish to emulate the technique that you're using. If people have a difficult time remembering their dreams, and frankly I'm such a person, what advice would you give?

Targ: Mainly, you want to separate out your residue of the previous day, which really clutters up your dream. You want to separate out your wish fulfillment, which makes up the other portion of people's usual dreams. Your dreams about what you would like to be, where you would like to go, you must separate them from those with surprising, bizarre characteristics. I don't know if I'm unusually good at that. Many people write down their dreams. They have whole books full of dreams, many psychologists, and many ESP researchers. I'm not one of those. I'm not that kind of researcher. It's just recently that I got particularly interested in precognition.

But my idea, in a nutshell, and which we'll come back to, is that in precognition, by and large, your sleeping brain is getting a signal from your awake brain. It's having an experience. If I have a dream of a naked person in a store window, and I wake up and I can see that naked person in the window, I now expect that sometime in the next day or next hour I'm going to see that picture on my [computer] screen or I'm going to be there. [in person] My wide-awake brain at ten o'clock is in communication with the sleeping brain. I would like to say that they're entangled, because that's a very current way of describing them. Three people just got Nobel Prizes for showing that things are indeed entangled. I don't know if the brain is quantum mechanically entangled.

Guy Playfair wrote a book about the shared experience of twins, *Twin Telepathy*, a very interesting book. He said, "The thing that made me want to write this book is that in London a man was shot dead on the street corner, and a mile away his brother fell to the pavement." He had a whole book of events like that. The brother, of course, wasn't shot and didn't hear the shot: they were separated by a mile. But he has a whole book full of events where twin A has usually some shocking experience and twin B experiences it or gets sick at the same time or has pain at the same time. It's crystal clear that the twins are entangled.

There's an American book about twin studies from Minneapolis, the Twin Cities, where they were bringing people from all over that neighborhood. The famous one that even made it to *Scientific American*, were the two brothers, both named James, who were identical twins but separated at birth. For religious reasons, they had to go to different places. But as they grew up it eventually came to pass that both became firemen, both married women named Linda, whom they then divorced and married women named Mary. They then showed up at the University of Minnesota wearing the same blue chambray shirt, steel rimmed glasses, and were happy to talk about their careers as firemen. I must assume that these two guys were entangled in some way. I'm just telling you what I remember from this whole article full of things they did in common, surprising everybody, enough to make it into *Scientific American*.

Playfair's book is full of events like that. The twins who had not seen each other for decades show up wearing the same dress from the same store. With the current vocabulary of quantum mechanics, I would say that their consciousness is entangled. You don't have to use that fraught word, but it's the idea. These identical twins show that they are somehow strongly connected. My hypothesis, here, is that your waking brain and your sleeping brain are entangled, much the same way as the brains of the twins. That's my going-in hypothesis. Does that make any sense to you?

Mishlove: It seems as if the similarity of the physical DNA, or even other features of the physical structure of the brain, has something to do with the possibility of telepathic communication, or, as you suggest, possibly entanglement. Naturally, what could be more similar than one's brain in the present and one's brain at some future time? It makes sense that they would be entangled. But then the question is, why at this time? Possibly, the events that we precognize in our dreams may have some significant emotional meaning. A Jungian interpretation would suggest that when a synchronicity occurs—and this could be viewed as a synchronicity—that there's something deeper behind it.

Targ: I had a dream about the Esalen Institute where I had lectured for almost forty years on psychic stuff. I would do weekend workshops. Finally in 2012, since I didn't know what was happening there, as a scientist I began to feel embarrassed about the lectures. It's like doing magic. I could demonstrate this stuff, show them how remote viewing works, but I had nothing to say about the mechanism. I got tired of displaying my ignorance year after year. So, I said goodbye to Mike Murphy and have not been there [Esalen] for almost twenty years.

Then I had a dream about being in the Big House, which is a large community building where we would all sit together in a circle; very pleasant. All the scientists or psychic researchers [were] in this very comfortable place on the hillside above the Pacific Ocean; lovely, wonderful vibrations. I hadn't been there for twenty years. Then I had a dream that I wanted to be with my friends again, but I couldn't afford the money to cross the river. It was sort of like you were locked out of heaven or something. I told Patty about this and she said, "If you want to go to Esalen, we can afford to go to Esalen. It's expensive but we can do that for a weekend if you want to." We let it go because I'm not that eager to go to Esalen; it's a bit of a long drive, and so forth.

So, I come into this room where I am now, with my cup of coffee as I do every day, [and] turn on my computer to see what's there. I had an email from Jeffrey Kripal, the professor of religion at Rice University, a pretty good friend of mine. I said, "Oh, what does Jeffrey have to say?" I opened his message to me, and a film started rolling, opening with a group of people sitting in the Big House, including me.

Russell Targ with parapsychological colleagues at the Esalen
Institute, Big Sur, California.

So, I pushed the button on my screen and the first thing I saw was a
whole group of people sitting in a circle at Esalen including myself. Five
minutes later, I told Patricia that's what I had in my dream. That's the
world I'm currently living in.

Mishlove: I believe Jeffrey Kripal is Chairman of the Board of Esalen
right now.

Targ: He wrote a book about Esalen and featured things that I had done
there and the teaching I had done at Esalen. I made it into his book.

Mishlove: But that's a very direct example, five minutes into the future,
of an unusual event. It was so unusual that you made a point of telling
Patty about it, which in your case is a very important criterion, otherwise
it wouldn't have counted.

Targ: That's right. I loved Esalen. It had a big emotional meaning for
me. It was not a wish fulfillment dream. I wasn't longing to be at Esalen,
or maybe in my subconscious I was. In a similar kind of dream.

I had a dream in which a Marklin electric train was running in a
circle around my living room. As a child, I was an aficionado of trains.
I had lots of trains in my life, but I never happened to own a Marklin.
The Marklin trains are interesting because they're very square backed,

like the elevated trains in Chicago. I told Patty I had a dream about electric toy trains running around our living room. She said, "Well, that's interesting; you've never had trains in this house as far as I know." I've been in the house for fifty years and never had any trains.

So, I took my coffee, turned on the *New York Times* and the front-page story for some reason was the rebuilding of the elevated trains in downtown Chicago, located right above my father's book shop on Dearborn Street. They show a very crisp picture of the train running in a circle around downtown Chicago, an area that's called The Loop. That had all sorts of hooks for me: connected to my father; connected to where I grew up in Chicago. I rode the elevated trains all the time. The dream was related to trains that I sort of hankered after, but never owned, namely fancy German trains. But again, it couldn't have been more than twenty minutes after I woke up when I told Patty about the trains running around our house; when I saw that on my screen.

Elevated train in Chicago.

Mishlove: I suppose that if—which I'm not—but, if I were to take a critical attitude towards this experiment, I might say, well, it could be that once you've had the dream and you discover that it's so unusual, now you're on the lookout to find something in your environment to match the dream. I think this is a very interesting experiment or experience that you're having. I imagine you would agree that it's not ready for publication yet in the IEEE journal [Institute of Electrical and Electronics Engineers Journal].

Targ: That's right, because we don't know what's going on. But the connection is usually very sharp.

Mishlove: In the last six months, how many of these successful precognitive dreams would you say there have been?

Targ: I've sent you four, and I would say there are two others that are, in a way, too elaborate to go into.

I think what's interesting about these dreams—I have a book now that's written from the future. I'm telling you, not about my crazy acid trip where I was making love to a snowman, but in this case, I have a dream that I tell somebody about in detail and then it occurs. That's what we usually require in a scientific experiment.

Now, the pumpkin dream is my favorite. You'll see why that is. All of these are very vivid dreams—I had a dream where I was with my wife Patricia, and she was dragging a huge pig on a leash down the street. She had a huge gray pig that she was dragging down the street. As you've caught on, now, that's probably a candidate for a possible precognitive dream. I loved it because it was such a weird, peculiar, out-of-context dream.

I went shuffling in my pajamas—Patti is always up before me, sitting with the coffee and the TV on over her head. I said, "I had this amazing dream about you dragging a huge pig." She said, "Well, if you look at the TV screen right over my head, you'll see there was this huge pumpkin in the back of a truck." I played the part of Mr. Magoo in this. I said, "Oh yeah, I see that huge pig with his tail sticking out." She laughed because it was not a pig at all: it was a one-ton pumpkin that just won a prize at the fair. It was a large one-ton pumpkin with its stalk sticking out the back.

Pumpkin

If you realize that Targ does not see very well, especially without his glasses at seven o'clock in the morning, Patti could tease me this way and say, "Yes, here's your pig," but it was a pumpkin that had just won a pumpkin prize.

The reason that I think it's a hot event for me is that it shows my dream is caused by what I apprehend, more than what was there. There was not a pig for me to see. Because of my bad vision and my wife's joke, I was perfectly ready to accept that there was a pig in the truck. It was really a pumpkin. When I had this dream, I did not dream about a Halloween pumpkin. I dreamt about the pig that I imagined I saw in the back of the truck. I thought, this is very circumstantial. The dream is, in fact, caused by what I see or think I see.

Mishlove: Would you say that in your dream you were looking at the pig from the rear end seeing the tail stick out the way it appears in this image of the pumpkin?

Targ: No, I would not. In the dream Patty was dragging it like a big dog down the street. But it looked like a big pig. My apprehension is that she was dragging a pig. When you show the image, you'll see that it looks like a pig, or a pumpkin, depending on what your apprehension is. Anyway, because of the misapprehension, I thought this a particularly good example of me showing that I'm not dreaming about what was out there but about what I think that I see.

The one that I think is the best and most interesting—because often these things show up in *The New York Times*—I had a dream about looking at a full page of *The New York Times* in print, which I can't read without my bifocals, and, certainly, people almost never read anything in a dream. But it was being narrated to me. This is a long story about the famous European Impressionist painter, Picasso. When I woke up I had the idea that this might be my favorite existentialist, Jean-Paul Sartre. Sartre occupies a sizable place in my cognition.

When I woke up, I thought this might be an article about Sartre, but I didn't tell Patty that. I said, "I had a dream about a French Impressionist whose picture appears in *The New York Times*. I feel very confident that he's really going to be there. So, instead of having my story just appear, I want you to come and share the experience with me." So, Patty and I sat together. I opened *The New York Times*, hit the button to show the picture, and there was a full-page picture of Pablo Picasso filling the page. Not only did I have the idea that it was indeed a European Impressionist, but I was so confident I was willing to call in Patty to share the experience of seeing it pop up. That demonstration of confidence makes me feel that I'm really making some progress about the signal-to-noise ratio of a future event.

You've got to remember, all these stories that I'm telling you about were things that manifested in my life but first appeared in a dream of the future. All these things that I'm seeing—Pablo Picasso in the *Times*—was half an hour before he appeared in my life. I think it's increasingly evident now that the future is available.

Mishlove: The future is available. That is a very interesting way of looking at life. We often imagine ourselves living along one timeline from birth to death, as we grow older, punctuated by certain events like marriage and other celebrations, vacations and so forth. It suggests that we're living in more than one dimension of time.

Targ: Oh, definitely. We misapprehend the whole nature of what's going on. You recall, the high point of my ESP career, after leaving SRI, was forecasting changes in the silver commodity market. I didn't do the forecasting, of course, but I set the stage using Stephan Schwartz's scheme of associative remote viewing. We know that remote viewers generally can't read the numbers on the big board in New York City. He can't see what silver is going to do. I couldn't say, "Look at the big board in New York and tell me what's going to happen there." But we can make an association. The broker has the job of deciding if silver will go up or silver will go down, or will it go up a little, or down a lot. He must choose from four possibilities each Monday. He could choose an object that corresponds to up a little, up a lot, down a little, or down a lot. It's a random association.

For example, he might say, this week if it goes up a lot, I'll show you the coffee cup. If it goes up a little, I'll show you the flowers. If it goes down a little, I'll show you my Swiss Army knife. If it goes down a lot, I'll show you my leftover pancake. Now, these objects, of course, have nothing to do with up or down, a little or a lot. Then I would sit with my friend Keith Harary, a prodigiously excellent psychic, lifelong psychic, who agreed to take part in the experiment with me.

So, on a typical Monday, Harary and I are sitting at my dining room table. I say, "Okay, Keith, here we are. We don't talk about silver at all. We're not forecasting anything." All Harary is asked to do by me, "Quiet your mind and tell me. I'm going to put something in your hand next Friday. I'd like you to tell me now what you experience. I'm going to find an interesting, unusual object, and I'll put it right in your hand, right here, right at my table. Tell me what surprising images come to your mind. What shows up regarding what I'm going to hand you next Friday?"

Keith might say, "You have something round and kind of floppy, and it has a bad smell. I don't really like this object." I would say, "That's a terrific description, unique. I think that's so unique that you can go now, and I'll see you next Friday." So, I called the broker. I said, "What have you got, John?" He said, "I've got my Swiss Army knife, and I got a cup of coffee, I got some flowers, and I've got my leftover pancake." I said, "Tell me about your leftover pancake." He said, "It was a regular pancake, leftover, round, and floppy. Based on the four objects that we had available, your friend Harary described the pancake much more clearly than any of the other four objects, obviously, and it's clear enough. I'm willing to go ahead."

Because Harary described the pancake very clearly, we would sell $20,000 worth of silver into what happened to be a rising market. The market went down that day, and we made our biggest hit of the series of nine trials, selling silver against the Hunt Brothers, because Harary saw a pancake instead of a coffee cup. We did that [for] nine weeks in a row. Harary described the correct object nine out of nine times. Our broker John exercised that forecast seven out of the nine times.

Two of the nine, of Harary's forecasts, although correct, deviated too much from what the experienced broker wanted to do. We're putting $50,000-$60,000 worth of cash into the market from an investor, and the broker has some feelings of responsibility. He really doesn't want to make a stupid investment based on a pancake, because he wouldn't have anything to tell his investor for why he lost $50,000, in this trial. So, we had nine forecasts all correct. Seven investments in the market, all correct. We made a quarter million dollars based on Harary's precognitive assessment of what he was going to have in his hand on the next Friday.

Mishlove: That's excellent evidence for precognition. I know that experiment was done back in the 1980s, almost forty years ago, Russell.

Targ: 1982.

Mishlove: More than forty years ago. Looking back over the last four decades, there have been many other efforts to replicate what you've done: some successful, some not. Do you have any feelings about the use of precognition to make money?

Targ: There's a group you know, the International Remote Viewing Association, IRVA, which is not a research organization, but an application. They are helping police find missing children in kidnap cases and making money in the market. Many of the IRVA people are using this associated remote viewing scheme to forecast sporting events, which gives you a chance to double your money. If your odds of being correct are pretty good odds, when forecasting sporting events, and you do it correctly, you'll double your money. There are quite a few people who claim to be making a living doing this now.

Mishlove: I'm under the impression that the successful ones don't like to talk about it too much.

Targ: Not publicly. People are willing to tell me what they're doing. They feel that they're happy that the ARV scheme, invented by Schwartz, and the fact that I made a ton of money forecasting gave some reality to these events.

Mishlove: Of course, it's well known at this point that there was a subsequent trial where, if I recall correctly, you lost nine times in a row.

Targ: The investor wanted to do this twice a week instead of once a week. "We've cornered the silver market; we're going to make a fortune."

Doing it twice a week instead of once a week means that the viewer does not get feedback for trial one until he's done trial two. We think that feedback is very important. We deprived the viewer of his feedback because that's what the investor wanted to do. The other thing we were doing was having me do the judging. I would judge from a tape recording left on my telephone. I had no credibility for being a judge, at all. I misjudged the first trial. Remote viewing judging requires skill.

In a nutshell, on the first trial, which I failed to judge, Harary said, "I think there's a zoo; I can smell the zoo, I see the animals," blah, blah, blah. Then he said, "No, it's not the zoo, it's an entertainment thing where you ride little cars around in a circle." That was the end of his recording. It turned out that one of the possibilities was a zoo; the other was a game, where you ride your car around in a circle. He had described two possible targets excellently. In our general view, in the case of ties, you choose the first one he described. That was not the right thing to do. It was the second thing he described. Harary was very angry about that, because he said to me, "If you listen to the tape, when I'm done with the zoo, I say clearly, this is not the target. The target is this riding game. If you were listening to me, you would have been correct." And that's all true. So, we decided that I'm not a good judge. This was not a good protocol and we dropped the experiment.

Mishlove: I guess it's fair to say that if someone wishes to engage in this kind of work to make money, they need to really treat it as a professional project because it's a very delicate process.

Targ: That's right. Our protocol was excellent. We know that feedback is very important. We dropped the feedback because that's what the investor wanted to do. We had the judging done by somebody who doesn't know anything about judging, which is me, in this case. We screwed up the experiment in several ways. It failed. But, since then, a few people have done this exact thing, and appear to be able to make money.

Mishlove: I wanted to refer to the work at Princeton that you alluded to before we began. The program where they did a lot of remote viewing exercises—experiments—and determined that the precognitive remote viewing worked just as well as real-time.

Targ: They published in one paper all the data for 334 trials, over a period of twenty years, significant at 10 to the minus 11th power. Looking into the future is no more difficult than looking into the distance.

Mishlove: The real question, and I guess we probably don't have a good answer yet, is radio signals for example, fall off with distance. Does remote viewing fall off as the distance becomes great, or in time does it fall off?

Targ: There's no evidence that remote viewing falls off with distance. No evidence at all. For example, one of the last things we did with Ingo Swann, our great remote viewer who invented the idea of remote viewing. We had a contract from NASA to test people's ability to learn with the ESP game. One day our contract monitor from NASA came to visit. He looked at the game, saw people really learning, which they were, and he turned to Ingo and said, "We're about to send Pioneer 2 to Jupiter. Would you like to look at Jupiter and tell us now whether we're going to find anything new there that people haven't seen before? Could you do that, Ingo?" He goes, "Yeah, I could do that. Give me a pencil and paper. I'll make you a drawing."

He made a drawing and said, "Basically, what's new about Jupiter is it has a couple of very large rings all the way around the planet. I don't believe anybody's ever seen large rings around Jupiter." Our friend, the administrator, said, "Aren't you thinking of Saturn?" Ingo says, "I spent my entire life looking at the solar system. You must believe I can tell the difference between Jupiter and Saturn."

Seven months later, the spacecraft got to Jupiter. In fact, the one thing it had to announce that was new was there are a couple of very large rings around Jupiter.

Ring discovered around Jupiter, as seen by Ingo Swann remote viewing months earlier.

Jupiter is 500 million miles away. The reason it's important is it took Ingo zero time to focus his attention on Jupiter and describe what was there. Now, 500 million miles away means that it's more than forty light minutes away. Assuming Ingo was using a physical property to view Jupiter, it would have taken him forty minutes to get any kind of electromagnetic signal from Jupiter to him. The important thing about this experiment, which I believe nobody has ever talked about, is that Ingo did a remote viewing faster than the speed of light.

Mishlove: It would certainly make sense if we can look into the future, and into the past as well—I know you have research pointing in that direction—then the speed of light becomes somewhat irrelevant.

Targ: Well, quantum physicists are very upset. All quantum physicists agree that you can't use quantum physics to send messages. They observe, correctly, [that] if you send messages with quantum physics, the messages will be transmitted faster than the speed of light or instantaneously. It's a true holy cow in modern physics: you cannot do anything faster than the speed of light. It's equally forbidden to look into the future. But the prima facie evidence of faster than the speed of light is particularly upsetting. All these things where you have one guy entangled with another one sending him messages about the future, is a big problem for modern physics.

Elizabeth Rauscher and I had a model of how that works. Elizabeth Rauscher was a physics professor at Berkeley, who died about a year ago. The model said that the space-time we live in is a complex space-time made up of real parts and imaginary parts. The consequence of this is [that] there will always be a trajectory from where you are to any other point in space-time. Because you have real parts and imaginary parts, there will always be a trajectory of zero distance between you and the distant place.

First, the good news is that it does not generate bad physics. You're not violating Maxwell's equations or Relativity theory because nothing is going, a priori, faster than the speed of light. You're following a path where there is no distance. There will always be a path where there is no distance. Basically, it's like you have a right triangle where one of the sides is imaginary. Where x squared plus y squared will give you a negative side and the distance will turn out to be zero. It is nothing more than the Pythagorean theorem that allows the distance to go to zero.

Mishlove: That makes perfect sense mathematically, Russell. It also suggests—and I know you're a deep student of Buddhism and various forms of meditation—it also suggests, if the distance between me and any other point in the universe is zero, that in some sense we are one with everything.

Targ: The Buddha said, again and again, there is no separation in consciousness. I don't know that he said there's no separation in anything. The idea of no separation in consciousness is in the *Prajnaparamita*, his writings. It's clear, as far as he's concerned, that human beings are not separated from one another. That's his clear pronouncement. This takes us back to where we began the discussion today, with the identical twins who essentially have a shared consciousness or a shared brain. I think everybody should read Guy Playfair's book, *Twin Telepathy*. Absolutely fascinating book. Playfair is a trustworthy English parapsychologist.

Mishlove: I would agree. That book, and in fact anything by Guy Lyon Playfair, is worth reading. Well, Russell, I want to thank you once again very much for being with me. I think that this is our sixteenth interview, as a matter of fact. I hope we can do many more.

Targ: Thank you very much for the opportunity. I appreciate your excellent interviewing. Thank you, Jeffrey.

Appendix – *Nature, Scientific Journal:* Vol. 251
October 18, 1974

Legon poses, as a challenge, the problem of obtaining work from the mixing of two ideal gases in an isolated system of constant total volume. It is elementary that if the mixture is allowed to form by merely withdrawing a partition between the gases we have a good example of a completely irreversible process with maximal entropy creation ($+11.53$ J K^{-1} if we started with 1 mol of each at 300 K) and no performance or storage of work. On the other hand, by introducing into the system a suitable machine, the uniform mixture could be allowed to form in such a way that a weight within the system was raised. (The machine described by Planck (ref. 8, page 219) may be readily adapted for this purpose.) At the end of the latter mixing process the isolated system would accordingly contain more mechanical energy than it did at the beginning. From the First Law it follows that the system must necessarily contain less thermal energy; that is, its temperature must have fallen. In the limit, where the mixing was reversible, the maximum possible work would have been performed and transferred to the weight (2,769 J if the gases were monatomic) and the temperature would have fallen to 189 K. In this reversible case the change in entropy arising from mixing ($+11.53$ J K^{-1}) is exactly counterbalanced by that attributable to cooling (-11.53 J K^{-1}): no entropy is created.

At this point it might be objected that the change in the gases is not exactly the same as if they had mixed irreversibly, because their thermal energy and temperature have decreased. This is a simple consequence of the First Law which applies equally no matter whether one is considering an isolated system, a non-isolated one or the whole Universe. If a change is conducted in such a way that a weight is lifted then all the other bodies involved cannot possibly end up in the same state as if the weight had not been lifted.

Failure to apply to nonisothermal systems. Legon expresses doubts about the validity of the equation for entropy creation (refs 3 and 4) save for "the trivial case for which the temperature T_e of the environment is equal to the temperature T of the system throughout the process"[2]. On what grounds are these doubts based? Legon does not discuss, let alone dismiss, any of the sources quoted in my article[5]. Other relevant sources which should be considered are Keenan and Hatsopoulos[13] and the classic accounts by Maxwell[10] and by Gouy[14].

Legon's quotation from Planck (ref. 8, page 104) concerning "dissipated energy" deserves close consideration. It seems to state that the maximum work is a definite quantity only for isothermal processes. If true this would directly contradict the views of Thomson[11] (later Lord Kelvin) "On a universal tendency in Nature to the dissipation of mechanical energy". On pages 113–117 of ref. 8, however, Planck discusses his own statement (ref. 8, page 104) and we see that there is in fact no contradiction. What Planck demonstrates is that although the change in Helmholtz free energy, $-dA = -d(U - TS)$, measures w_{max} under isothermal conditions, it cannot conveniently be used to determine w_{max} under nonisothermal conditions because the term S dT that then appears is frequently indeterminate. The same point has already been made in a footnote by Gouy (ref. 15, page 506) who had also given the correct equation for determining w_{max} under nonisothermal conditions. Accordingly I find no substance in Legon's objections under this heading.

If it is thought that there is conflict between the 'work' view of thermodynamics and the 'entropy' view it is high time that the idea was abandoned. The two views are different, but symmetrical, aspects of the same reality. Spontaneous processes of all kinds fall somewhere within the pattern shown in Table 1, their position depending on the efficiency of the machinery used for the extraction of work.

D. R. Wilkie

Department of Physiology,
University College London,
Gower Street,
London WC1E 6BT, UK

Received December 3, 1973; revised June 4, 1974.

1 Bridgman, P. W., *The Nature of Thermodynamics*, 116 (Harvard University Press, Cambridge, Massachusetts, 1943).
2 Everett, D. H.. *Chemical Thermodynamics*, 216 (Longman, London, 1971).
3 Legon, A. C., *Nature*, **244**, 431 (1973).
4 Wilkie, D. R., *Nature*, **242**, 606 (1973).
5 Wilkie, D. R., *Nature*, **245**, 457 (1973).
6 Butler, J. A. V., *Chemical Thermodynamics*, fourth ed. (Macmillan, 1955).
7 Carnot, S., *Reflections on the motive power of fire* (1824), translation (Dover, New York, 1960).
8 Planck, M., *Treatise on Thermodynamics*, third ed., trans. from seventh German ed., 1922 (Dover, New York, 1958).
9 Joule, J. P., *Phil. Mag.*, Series 4, **5**, 1 (1853).
10 Maxwell, J. C., *Theory of Heat*, fifth ed., chapter XII (Longmans Green, London, 1877).
11 Thomson, W., *Phil. Mag.*, Series 4, **5**, 102 (1853).
12 Guggenheim, E. A., *Thermodynamics*, third ed. (North Holland, Amsterdam, 1957).
13 Keenan, J. H., and Hatsopoulos, G. N., *Principles of General Thermodynamics* (Wiley, New York, 1965).
14 Gouy, M., J. *de Phys.*, 2ᵉ série, t.VIII (Novembre 1889).
15 Thomson, W., *Phil. Mag.*, Series 4, **4**, 304 (1852); corrections in *ibid*, **5**, viii.

Information transmission under conditions of sensory shielding

We present results of experiments suggesting the existence of one or more perceptual modalities through which individuals obtain information about their environment, although this information is not presented to any known sense. The literature[1-3] and our observations lead us to conclude that such abilities can be studied under laboratory conditions.

We have investigated the ability of certain people to describe graphical material or remote scenes shielded against ordinary perception. In addition, we performed pilot studies to determine if electroencephalographic (EEG) recordings might indicate perception of remote happenings even in the absence of correct overt responses.

We concentrated on what we consider to be our primary responsibility—to resolve under conditions as unambiguous as possible the basic issue of whether a certain class of paranormal perception phenomena exists. So we conducted our experiments with sufficient control, utilising visual, acoustic and electrical shielding, to ensure that all conventional paths of sensory input were blocked. At all times we took measures to prevent sensory leakage and to prevent deception, whether intentional or unintentional.

Our goal is not just to catalogue interesting events, but to uncover patterns of cause–effect relationships that lend themselves to analysis and hypothesis in the forms with which we are familiar in scientific study. The results presented here constitute a first step towards that goal; we have established under known conditions a data base from which departures as a function of physical and psychological variables can be studied in future work.

REMOTE PERCEPTION OF GRAPHIC MATERIAL

First, we conducted experiments with Mr Uri Geller in which we examined his ability, while located in an electrically shielded room, to reproduce target pictures drawn by experimenters located at remote locations. Second, we conducted double-blind experiments with Mr Pat Price, in which we measured his ability to describe remote outdoor scenes many miles from his physical location. Finally, we conducted pre-

Nature Vol. 251 October 18 1974

603

liminary tests using EEGs, in which subjects were asked to perceive whether a remote light was flashing, and to determine whether a subject could perceive the presence of the light, even if only at a noncognitive level of awareness.

In preliminary testing Geller apparently demonstrated an ability to reproduce simple pictures (line drawings) which had been drawn and placed in opaque sealed envelopes which he was not permitted to handle. But since each of the targets was known to at least one experimenter in the room with Geller, it was not possible on the basis of the preliminary testing to discriminate between Geller's direct perception of envelope contents and perception through some mechanism involving the experimenters, whether paranormal or subliminal.

So we examined the phenomenon under conditions designed to eliminate all conventional information channels, overt or subliminal. Geller was separated from both the target material and anyone knowledgeable of the material, as in the experiments of ref. 4.

In the first part of the study a series of 13 separate drawing experiments were carried out over 7 days. No experiments are deleted from the results presented here.

At the beginning of the experiment either Geller or the experimenters entered a shielded room so that from that time forward Geller was at all times visually, acoustically and electrically shielded from personnel and material at the target location. Only following Geller's isolation from the experimenters was a target chosen and drawn, a procedure designed to eliminate pre-experiment cueing. Furthermore, to eliminate the possibility of pre-experiment target forcing, Geller was kept ignorant as to the identity of the person selecting the target and as to the method of target selection. This was accomplished by the use of three different techniques: (1) pseudo-random technique of opening a dictionary arbitrarily and choosing the first word that could be drawn (Experiments 1–4); (2) targets, blind to experimenters and subject, prepared independently by

SRI scientists outside the experimental group (following Geller's isolation) and provided to the experimenters during the course of the experiment (Experiments 5–7, 11–13); and (3) arbitrary selection from a target pool decided upon in advance of daily experimentation and designed to provide data concerning information content for use in testing specific hypotheses (Experiments 8–10). Geller's task was to reproduce with pen on paper the line drawing generated at the target location. Following a period of effort ranging from a few minutes to half an hour, Geller either passed (when he did not feel confident) or indicated he was ready to submit a drawing to the experimenters, in which case the drawing was collected before Geller was permitted to see the target.

To prevent sensory cueing of the target information, Experiments 1 through 10 were carried out using a shielded room in SRI's facility for EEG research. The acoustic and visual isolation is provided by a double-walled steel room, locked by means of an inner and outer door, each of which is secured with a refrigerator-type locking mechanism. Following target selection when Geller was inside the room, a one-way audio monitor, operating only from the inside to the outside, was activated to monitor Geller during his efforts. The target picture was never discussed by the experimenters after the picture was drawn and brought near the shielded room. In our detailed examination of the shielded room and the protocol used in these experiments, no sensory leakage has been found.

The conditions and results for the 10 experiments carried out in the shielded room are displayed in Table 1 and Fig. 1. All experiments except 4 and 5, were conducted with Geller inside the shielded room. In Experiments 4 and 5, the procedure was reversed. For those experiments in which Geller was inside the shielded room, the target location was in an adjacent room at a distance of about 4 m, except for Experiments 3 and 8, in which the target locations were, respectively, an office at a distance of 475 m and a room at a distance of about 7 m.

A response was obtained in all experiments except Numbers 5–7. In Experiment 5, the person-to-person link was eliminated by arranging for a scientist outside the usual experimental group to draw a picture, lock it in the shielded room before Geller's arrival at SRI, and leave the area. Geller was then led

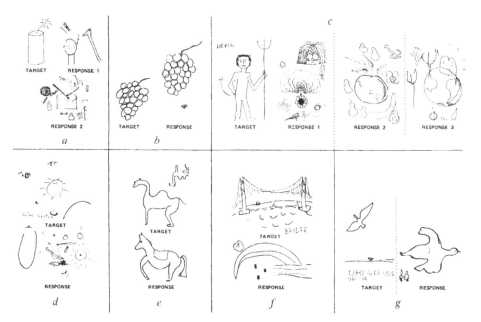

Fig. 1 Target pictures and responses drawn by Uri Geller under shielded conditions.

Table 1 Remote perception of graphic material

Experiment	Date (month, day, year)	Geller Location	Target Location	Target	Figure
1	8/4/73	Shielded room 1*	Adjacent room (4.1 m)†	Firecracker	1a
2	8/4/73	Shielded room 1	Adjacent room (4.1 m)	Grapes	1b
3	8/5/73	Shielded room 1	Office (475 m)	Devil	1c
4	8/5/73	Room adjacent to shielded room 1	Shielded room 1 (3.2 m)	Solar system	1d
5	8/6/73	Room adjacent to shielded room 1	Shielded room 1 (3.2 m)	Rabbit	No drawing
6	8/7/73	Shielded room 1	Adjacent room (4.1 m)	Tree	No drawing
7	8/7/73	Shielded room 1	Adjacent room (4.1 m)	Envelope	No drawing
8	8/8/73	Shielded room 1	Remote room (6.75 m)	Camel	1e
9	8/8/73	Shielded room 1	Adjacent room (4.1 m)	Bridge	1f
10	8/8/73	Shielded room 1	Adjacent room (4.1 m)	Seagull	1g
11	8/9/73	Shielded room 2‡	Computer (54 m)	Kite (computer CRT)	2a
12	8/10/73	Shielded room 2	Computer (54 m)	Church (computer memory)	2b
13	8/10/73	Shielded room 2	Computer (54 m)	Arrow through heart (computer CRT, zero intensity)	2c

*EEG Facility shielded room (see text).
†Perceiver–target distances measured in metres.
‡SRI Radio Systems Laboratory shielded room (see text).

by the experimenters to the shielded room and asked to draw the picture located inside the room. He said that he got no clear impression and therefore did not submit a drawing. The elimination of the person-to-person link was examined further in the second series of experiments with this subject.

Experiments 6 and 7 were carried out while we attempted to record Geller's EEG during his efforts to perceive the target pictures. The target pictures were, respectively, a tree and an envelope. He found it difficult to hold adequately still for good EEG records, said that he experienced difficulty in getting impressions of the targets and again submitted no drawings.

Experiments 11 through 13 were carried out in SRI's Engineering Building, to make use of the computer facilities available there. For these experimenters, Geller was secured in a double-walled, copper-screen Faraday cage 54 m down the hall and around the corner from the computer room. The Faraday cage provides 120 dB attenuation for plane wave radio frequency radiation over a range of 15 kHz to 1 GHz. For magnetic fields the attenuation is 68 dB at 15 kHz and decreases to 3 dB at 60 Hz. Following Geller's isolation, the targets for these experiments were chosen by computer laboratory personnel not otherwise associated with either the experiment or Geller, and the experimenters and subject were kept blind as to the contents of the target pool.

For Experiment 11, a picture of a kite was drawn on the face of a cathode ray tube display screen, driven by the computer's graphics program. For Experiment 12, a picture of a church was drawn and stored in the memory of the computer. In Experiment 13, the target drawing, an arrow through a heart (Fig. 2c), was drawn on the face of the cathode ray tube and then the display intensity was turned off so that no picture was visible.

To obtain an independent evaluation of the correlation between target and response data, the experimenters submitted the data for judging on a 'blind' basis by two SRI scientists who were not otherwise associated with the research. For the 10 cases in which Geller provided a response, the judges were asked to match the response data with the corresponding target data (without replacement). In those cases in which Geller made more than one drawing as his response to the target, all the drawings were combined as a set for judging. The two judges each matched the target data to the response data with no error. For either judge such a correspondence has an *a priori* probability, under the null hypothesis of no information channel, of $P = (10!)^{-1} = 3 \times 10^{-7}$.

A second series of experiments was carried out to determine whether direct perception of envelope contents was possible without some person knowing of the target picture.

One hundred target pictures of everyday objects were drawn by an SRI artist and sealed by other SRI personnel in double envelopes containing black cardboard. The hundred targets were divided randomly into groups of 20 for use in each of the three days' experiments.

On each of the three days of these experiments, Geller passed. That is, he declined to associate any envelope with a drawing that he made, expressing dissatisfaction with the existence of such a large target pool. On each day he made approximately 12 recognisable drawings, which he felt were associated with the entire target pool of 100. On each of the three days, two of his drawings could reasonably be associated with two of the 20 daily targets. On the third day, two of his drawings were very close replications of two of that day's target pictures. The drawings resulting from this experiment do not depart significantly from what would be expected by chance.

In a simpler experiment Geller was successful in obtaining information under conditions in which no persons were knowledgeable of the target. A double-blind experiment was performed in which a single 3/4 inch die was placed in a $3 \times 4 \times 5$ inch steel box. The box was then vigorously shaken by one of the experimenters and placed on the table, a technique found in control runs to produce a distribution of die faces differing nonsignificantly from chance. The orientation of the die within the box was unknown to the experimenters at that time. Geller would then write down which die face was uppermost. The target pool was known, but the targets were individually prepared in a manner blind to all persons involved in the experiment. This experiment was performed ten times, with Geller passing twice and giving a response eight times. In the eight times in which he gave a response, he was correct each time. The distribution of responses consisted of three 2s, one 4, two 5s, and two 6s. The probability of this occurring by chance is approximately one in 10^6.

In certain situations significant information transmission can take place under shielded conditions. Factors which appear to be important and therefore candidates for future investigation include whether the subject knows the set of targets in the target pool, the actual number of targets in the target pool at any given time, and whether the target is known by any of the experimenters.

It has been widely reported that Geller has demonstrated the ability to bend metal by paranormal means. Although metal bending by Geller has been observed in our laboratory, we have not been able to combine such observations with adequately controlled experiments to obtain data sufficient to support the paranormal hypothesis.

REMOTE VIEWING OF NATURAL TARGETS

A study by Osis[5] led us to determine whether a subject could describe randomly chosen geographical sites located several miles from the subject's position and demarcated by some

Nature Vol. 251 October 18 1974

605

appropriate means (remote viewing). This experiment carried out with Price, a former California police commissioner and city councilman, consisted of a series of double-blind, demonstration-of-ability tests involving local targets in the San Francisco Bay area which could be documented by several independent judges. We planned the experiment considering that natural geographical places or man-made sites that have existed for a long time are more potent targets for paranormal perception experiments than are artificial targets prepared in the laboratory. This is based on subject opinions that the use of artificial targets involves a 'trivialisation of the ability' as compared with natural pre-existing targets.

In each of nine experiments involving Price as subject and SRI experimenters as a target demarcation team, a remote location was chosen in a double-blind protocol. Price, who remained at SRI, was asked to describe this remote location, as well as whatever activities might be going on there.

Several descriptions yielded significantly correct data pertaining to and descriptive of the target location.

In the experiments a set of twelve target locations clearly differentiated from each other and within 30 min driving time from SRI had been chosen from a target-rich environment (more than 100 targets of the type used in the experimental series) prior to the experimental series by an individual in SRI management, the director of the Information Science and Engineering Division, not otherwise associated with the experiment. Both

the experimenters and the subject were kept blind as to the contents of the target pool, which were used without replacement.

An experimenter was closeted with Price at SRI to wait 30 min to begin the narrative description of the remote location. The SRI locations from which the subject viewed the remote locations consisted of an outdoor park (Experiments 1, 2), the double-walled copper-screen Faraday cage discussed earlier (Experiments 3, 4, and 6-9), and an office (Experiment 5). A second experimenter would then obtain a target location from the Division Director from a set of travelling orders previously prepared and randomised by the Director and kept under his control. The target demarcation team (two to four SRI experimenters) then proceeded directly to the target by automobile without communicating with the subject or experimenter remaining behind. Since the experimenter remaining with the subject at SRI was in ignorance both as to the particular target and as to the target pool, he was free to question Price to clarify his description. The demarcation team then remained at the target site for 30 min after the 30 min allotted for travel. During the observation period, the remote-viewing subject would describe his impressions of the target site into a tape recorder. A comparison was then made when the demarcation team returned.

Price's ability to describe correctly buildings, docks, roads, gardens and so on, including structural materials, colour, ambience and activity, sometimes in great detail, indicated the functioning of a remote perceptual ability. But the descriptions contained inaccuracies as well as correct statements. To obtain a numerical evaluation of the accuracy of the remote viewing experiment, the experimental results were subjected to independent judging on a blind basis by five SRI scientists who were

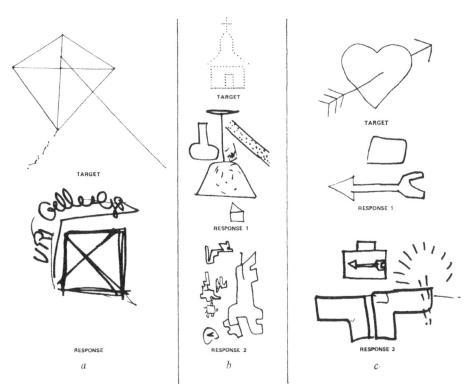

Fig. 2 Computer drawings and responses drawn by Uri Geller. *a*, Computer drawing stored on video display; *b*, computer drawing stored in computer memory only; *c*, computer drawing stored on video display with zero intensity.

Table 2 Distribution of correct selections by judges A, B, C, D, and E in remote viewing experiments

Descriptions chosen by judges		Places visited by judges								
		1	2	3	4	5	6	7	8	9
Hoover Tower	1	ABCDE				D				
Baylands Nature Preserve	2		ABC	E				D		D
Radio Telescope	3			ACD		BE				
Redwood City Marina	4		CD		ABDE		E			
Bridge Toll Plaza	5						ABD		DCE	
Drive-In Theatre	6		B			A	C			E
Arts and Crafts Garden Plaza	7							ABCE		
Church	8				C				AB	
Rinconada Park	9		CE							AB

Of the 45 selections (5 judges, 9 choices), 24 were correct. Bold type indicates the description chosen most often for each place visited. Correct choices lie on the main diagonal. The number of correct matches by Judges A through E is 7, 6, 5, 3, and 3, respectively. The expected number of correct matches from the five judges was five; in the experiment 24 such matches were obtained. The *a priori* probability of such an occurrence by chance, conservatively assuming assignment without replacement on the part of the judges, is $P = 8.10^{-10}$.

not otherwise associated with the research. The judges were asked to match the nine locations, which they independently visited, against the typed manuscripts of the tape-recorded narratives of the remote viewer. The transcripts were unlabelled and presented in random order. The judges were asked to find a narrative which they would consider the best match for each of the places they visited. A given narrative could be assigned to more than one target location. A correct match requires that the transcript of a given date be associated with the target of that date. Table 2 shows the distribution of the judges' choices.

Among all possible analyses, the most conservative is a permutation analysis of the plurality vote of the judges' selections assuming assignment without replacement, an approach independent of the number of judges. By plurality vote, six of the nine descriptions and locations were correctly matched. Under the null hypothesis (no remote viewing and a random selection of descriptions without replacement), this outcome has an *a priori* probability of $P = 5.6 \times 10^{-4}$, since, among all possible permutations of the integers one through nine, the probability of six or more being in their natural position in the list has that value. Therefore, although Price's descriptions contain inaccuracies, the descriptions are sufficiently accurate to permit the judges to differentiate among the various targets to the degree indicated.

EEG EXPERIMENTS

An experiment was undertaken to determine whether a physiological measure such as EEG activity could be used as an indicator of information transmission between an isolated subject and a remote stimulus. We hypothesised that perception could be indicated by such a measure even in the absence of verbal or other overt indicators.[6,7]

It was assumed that the application of remote stimuli would result in responses similar to those obtained under conditions of direct stimulation. For example, when normal subjects are stimulated with a flashing light, their EEG typically shows a decrease in the amplitude of the resting rhythm and a driving of the brain waves at the frequency of the flashes.[8] We hypothesised that if we stimulated one subject in this manner (a sender), the EEG of another subject in a remote room with no flash present (a receiver), might show changes in alpha (9–11 Hz) activity, and possibly EEG driving similar to that of the sender.

We informed our subject that at certain times a light was to be flashed in a sender's eyes in a distant room, and if the subject perceived that event, consciously or unconsciously, it might be evident from changes in his EEG output. The receiver was seated in the visually opaque, acoustically and electrically shielded double-walled steel room previously described. The sender was seated in a room about 7 m from the receiver.

To find subjects who were responsive to such a remote stimulus, we initially worked with four female and two male volunteer subjects, all of whom believed that success in the experimental situation might be possible. These were designated

'receivers'. The senders were either other subjects or the experimenters. We decided beforehand to run one or two sessions of 36 trials each with each subject in this selection procedure, and to do a more extensive study with any subject whose results were positive.

A Grass PS-2 photostimulator placed about 1 m in front of the sender was used to present flash trains of 10 s duration. The receiver's EEG activity from the occipital region (O_z), referenced to linked mastoids, was amplified with a Grass 5P-1 preamplifier and associated driver amplifier with a bandpass of 1–120 Hz. The EEG data were recorded on magnetic tape with an Ampex SP 300 recorder.

On each trial, a tone burst of fixed frequency was presented to both sender and receiver and was followed in one second by either a 10 s train of flashes or a null flash interval presented to the sender. Thirty-six such trials were given in an experimental session, consisting of 12 null trials—no flashes following the tone—12 trials of flashes at 6 f.p.s. and 12 trials of flashes at 16 f.p.s., all randomly intermixed, determined by entries from a table of random numbers. Each of the trials generated an 11-s EEG epoch. The last 4 s of the epoch was selected for analysis to minimise the desynchronising action of the warning cue. This 4-s segment was subjected to Fourier analysis on a LINC 8 computer.

Spectrum analyses gave no evidence of EEG driving in any receiver, although in control runs the receivers did exhibit driving when physically stimulated with the flashes. But of the six subjects studied initially, one subject (H. H.) showed a consistent alpha blocking effect. We therefore undertook further study with this subject.

Data from seven sets of 36 trials each were collected from this subject on three separate days. This comprises all the data collected to date with this subject under the test conditions described above. The alpha band was identified from average spectra, then scores of average power and peak power were obtained from individual trials and subjected to statistical analysis.

Of our six subjects, H. H. had by far the most monochromatic EEG spectrum. Figure 3 shows an overlay of the three averaged spectra from one of this subject's 36-trial runs, displaying changes in her alpha activity for the three stimulus conditions.

Mean values for the average power and peak power for each

Table 3 EEG data for H.H. showing average power and peak power in the 9–11 Hz band, as a function of flash frequency and sender

Flash Frequency	0	6	16	0	6	16
Sender	Average Power			Peak Power		
J.L.	94.8	84.1	76.8	357.7	329.2	289.6
R.T.	41.3	45.5	37.0	160.7	161.0	125.0
No sender (subject informed)	25.1	35.7	28.2	87.5	95.7	81.7
J.L.	54.2	55.3	44.8	191.4	170.5	149.3
J.L.	56.8	50.9	32.8	240.6	178.0	104.6
R.T.	39.8	24.9	30.3	145.2	74.2	122.1
No sender (subject not informed)	86.0	53.0	52.1	318.1	180.6	202.3
Averages	56.8	49.9	43.1	214.5	169.8	153.5
		-12%	$-24\%(P<0.04)$		-21%	$-28\%(P<0.03)$

Each entry is an average over 12 trials

Nature Vol. 251 October 18 1974

of the seven experimental sets are given in Table 3. The power measures were less in the 16 f.p.s. case than in the 0 f.p.s. in all seven peak power measures and in six out of seven average power measures. Note also the reduced effect in the case in which the subject was informed that no sender was present (Run 3). It seems that overall alpha production was reduced for this run in conjunction with the subject's expressed apprehension about conducting the experiment without a sender. This is in contrast to the case (Run 7) in which the subject was not informed.

Siegel's two-tailed t approximation to the nonparametric randomisation test[9] was applied to the data from all sets, which included two sessions in which the sender was removed. Average power on trials associated with the occurrence of 16 f.p.s. was significantly less than when there were no flashes ($t = 2.09$, d.f. $= 118$, $P < 0.04$). The second measure, peak power, was also significantly less in the 16 f.p.s. conditions than in the null condition ($t = 2.16$, d.f. $= 118$, $P < 0.03$). The average response in the 6 f.p.s. condition was in the same direction as that associated with 16 f.p.s., but the effect was not statistically significant.

Spectrum analyses of control recordings made from saline with a 12 kΩ resistance in place of the subject with and without the addition of a 10 Hz, 50 μV test signal applied to the saline solution, revealed no indications of flash frequencies, nor perturbations of the 10 Hz signal. These controls suggest that the results were not due to system artefacts. Further tests also gave no evidence of radio frequency energy associated with the stimulus.

Subjects were asked to indicate their conscious assessment for each trial as to which stimulus was generated. They made their guesses known to the experimenter via one-way telegraphic communication. An analysis of these guesses has shown them to be at chance, indicating the absence of any supraliminal cueing, so arousal as evidenced by significant alpha blocking occurred only at the noncognitive level of awareness.

We hypothesise that the protocol described here may prove to be useful as a screening procedure for latent remote perceptual ability in the general population.

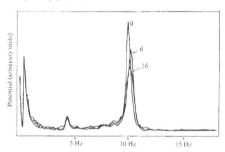

Fig. 3 Occipital EEG spectra, 0–20 Hz, for one subject (H. H.) acting as receiver, showing amplitude changes in the 9–11 Hz band as a function of strobe frequency. Three cases: 0, 6, and 16 f.p.s. (12 trial averages).

CONCLUSION

From these experiments we conclude that:
- A channel exists whereby information about a remote location can be obtained by means of an as yet unidentified perceptual modality.
- As with all biological systems, the information channel appears to be imperfect, containing noise along with the signal.
- While a quantitative signal-to-noise ratio in the information-theoretical sense cannot as yet be determined, the results of our experiments indicate that the functioning is at the level of useful information transfer.

It may be that remote perceptual ability is widely distributed in the general population, but because the perception is generally below an individual's level of awareness, it is repressed or not noticed. For example, two of our subjects (H. H. and P. P.) had not considered themselves to have unusual perceptual ability before their participation in these experiments.

Our observation of the phenomena leads us to conclude that

experiments in the area of so-called paranormal phenomena can be scientifically conducted, and it is our hope that other laboratories will initiate additional research to attempt to replicate these findings.

This research was sponsored by The Foundation for Parasensory Investigation, New York City. We thank Mrs Judith Skutch, Dr Edgar D. Mitchell of the Institute of Noetic Sciences—as well as our SRI associates, Mr Bonnar Cox, Mr Earle Jones and Dr Dean Brown—for support and encouragement. Constructive suggestions by Mrs Jean Mayo, Dr Charles Tart, University of California, and Dr Robert Ornstein and Dr David Galin of the Langley Porter Neuropsychiatric Institute are acknowledged.

RUSSELL TARG
HAROLD PUTHOFF

Electronics and Bioengineering Laboratory,
Stanford Research Institute,
Menlo Park, California 94025

Received March 11; revised July 8, 1974.

[1] Pratt, J., Rhine, J. B., Stuart, C., and Greenwood, J., *Extra Sensory Perception after Sixty Years* (Henry Holt, New York, 1940).
[2] Soal, S., and Bateman, F., *Modern Experiments in Telepathy* (Faber and Faber, London, 1954).
[3] Vasilliev, L. L., *Experiments in Mental Suggestion* (ISMI Publications, Hampshire, England, 1963).
[4] Musso, J. R., and Granero, M., *J. Parapsychology,* **37,** 13–37 (1973).
[5] Osis, K., *ASPR Newsletter,* No. 14 (1972).
[6] Tart, C. T., *Physiological Correlates of Psi Cognition, Int. J. Parapsychology,* **V,** No. 4 (1963).
[7] Dean, E. D., *Int. J. Neuropsychiatry,* **2** (1966).
[8] Hill, D., and Parr, G., *Electroencephalography : A Symposium on its Various Aspects* (Macmillan, New York, 1963).
[9] Siegel, S., *Nonparametric Statistics for the Behavioral Sciences,* 152–156 (McGraw-Hill, New York, 1956).

The stability of a feasible random ecosystem

THE weight of the evidence, and the beliefs of most biologists, seem to support the view[1] that ecosystems tend to be more stable, the larger the number of interacting species they contain. It is puzzling, therefore, that a variety of mathematical models of complex ecosystems appear to give the contrary answer: that complexity makes for instability[2].

Prominent among such models is the complex system with random interactions, studied in various forms by Gardner and Ashby[3] and May[4]; but their results cannot be applied as they stand to ecological systems. In an ecosystem, the interacting variables are species populations (or species biomass) which cannot take on negative values. Thus, for example, the equilibrium population values must be positive, and it is convenient to denote this necessary property of an ecosystem model by saying that it must be 'feasible'.

The work referred to imposed no such constraint on equilibrium populations in the samples considered. It is of some interest, therefore, to examine the stability of a random model capable of representing ecosystems, by imposing the restriction that the sample be feasible.

I report here the results of computer calculations on such a model. The interaction equations were of the well-known quasi-linear type, in which the rate of fractional increase of a species population is a linear function of the current populations in all T species. That is, the number N_i in the ith species obeys

$$dN_i/dt = N_i (b_i + \Sigma_j a_{ij} N_j).$$

All birth rates b_i were taken as 1, and the self-regulating coefficients a_{ii} as -1. The feasibility requirement was that the

Jeff in 2023

About the Author

*N*ew *Thinking Allowed* host, Jeffrey Mishlove, PhD, is author of *The Roots of Consciousness, Psi Development Systems, The PK Man*, and the *New Thinking Allowed Dialogues series: Is There Life After Death? UFOs and UAP: Are we Really Alone?* and *Russell Targ: Ninety Years of Remote Viewing, ESP, and Timeless Awareness*.

He is the recipient of the only doctoral diploma in the world from an accredited university that says, "Parapsychology." It was awarded from the University of California, Berkeley, in 1980. He is also the Grand Prize winner of the Bigelow Institute essay competition regarding postmortem survival of human consciousness.

Issue 05/Spring 2024
English Original Transcripts

Conversations on the Leading Edge
of Knowledge & Discovery

NEW THINKING
ALLOWED MAGAZINE

Quarterly Highlight
**Can We Harvest
Zero-Point Energy?**
Garret Moddel

*New Thinking Allowed
YouTube Interviews*
Whitley Strieber
Lyn Buchanan
Robert Bigelow
Elly Flippen

New Thinking Allowed TV series
Terence McKenna

MAGAZINE PUBLISHED BY THE NEW THINKING ALLOWED FOUNDATION

The New Thinking Allowed Foundation has recently launched a quarterly magazine. Copies can be downloaded for FREE from the New Thinking Allowed Foundation website, www.newthinkingallowed.org, and printed copies can be ordered from https://nta-magazine.magcloud.com